Page	Content
1	Your travelling companion to a more colourful life
2	What this book is about
3	The five element cycle
4	Meridians and how to work with them
5	The concept of yin and yang
6	About the author and the birth of this project
7	Central meridian insights
8	Space for reflection
9	Releasing and updating to keep up with the times
10	Developing respect for intelligence
11	Governing meridian insights
12	Space for reflection
13	Establishing core values
14	Be wide awake or fast asleep
15	Turn over a new leaf with wood element energy
16	Space for reflection
17	Liver meridian insights
18	Dispelling the taboo of anger
19	Spring clean your routine
20	How many hats do you wear?
21	Small steps to big changes
22	Take a chance → make a choice → change
23	Find your happy
24	Practical ways to support liver meridian energy
25	Gall bladder meridian insights
26	A bedtime story for grown ups
27	Motivation and where to find it
28	Paralysis by analysis and how to get out of it
29	Shift through the fog
30	Re-invent your life
31	Stepping stones out of overwhelm
32	Everyday support for gall bladder meridian energy
33	Spark up your fire, welcome joy & love into your life
34	Space for reflection
35	Heart meridian insights
36	Do you take things to heart?
37	On forgiveness
38	Fire up your passions
39	Joy & Gratitude
40	Follow your heart
41	Never underestimate the power of the hug
42	Stoke your fire with a riot of colour
43	Pericardium meridian insights
44	Power, strength and subtle energy
45	Preserving the gifts and mysteries
46	Updating the legacy
47	Seek silence, speak softly
48	Your vibe attracts your tribe
49	Give yourself permission to live
50	Heaven scent
51	Small intestine meridian insights
52	Develop your internal discernment
53	Digging for buried treasure
54	To do or not to do, that is the question
55	24 hour time planner
56	Work with small intestine energy - Let's do this
57	Break it down
58	Prioritise action
59	Triple warmer meridian insights
60	Break the habit

Contents

Page	Content
61	Good fences make great neighbours
62	Communicating and maintaining boundaries
63	Benefits of meditation and breath work
64	Know your heat
65	Pause for menopause
66	Tame your fire — restore your cool
67	Reap the harvest of all your efforts with earth element
68	Space for reflection
69	Spleen meridian insights
70	Dealing with toxic thoughts, behaviours and emotions
71	The truth about confidence
72	What if it all went right?
73	Wake up your immune system
74	Celebrate to accumulate
75	Nourishment for spleen meridian energy
76	Connect with the Earth
77	Stomach meridian insights
78	Nourish and glow
79	Heal your inner child
80	Embracing the child within
81	Simple hacks to support stomach meridian energy
82	Fulfilment and satisfaction
83	Look around
84	Monitor your hidden intake
85	Let go and breathe easy with metal element energy
86	Space for reflection
87	Lung meridian insights
88	Releasing weighty emotional armour
89	Stretch and glow
90	Complimentary jewels
91	Reading., writing and reality
92	The healing power of breath
93	Nourish lung meridian energy
94	Releasing regret
95	Large intestine meridian insights
96	Clean from the inside out
97	De-clutter your life
98	Would-a, should-a, could-a
99	Chase away the blues
100	Surviving depression
101	Loss and forgiveness
102	Feed your gut
103	Release fear and dream the dream of the future
104	Space for reflection
105	Kidney meridian insights
106	Embrace the frequency of water
107	Water, water, everywhere
108	Cleaning your internal storage space
109	The mystery of dreamtime
110	Keep calm & carry on
111	Who do you think you are?
112	Breathing and other simple kidney meridian hacks
113	Bladder meridian insights
114	Who's got your back?
115	Who gets a seat at your kitchen table?
116	Make friends with fear
117	Making resolutions that work
118	Simple bladder meridian hacks
119	Patience
120	Be patient, not a patient

What it is to live deliberately

To live deliberately is to live consciously and with intention. Being aware of our choices and the beliefs, habits and behaviours that drive them.

To live deliberately is to be present and engaged, every step of the way.

This colouring workbook helps explore your unconscious and bring awareness to intention. Think of it as your own personal companion, helping develop new tools and strategies to ease your journey, through your day, your year, and your life.

Learn to gracefully reveal and sustain your beautiful, authentic self, as you work harmoniously with subtle, powerful, natural energies.

Silence your habitual inner critic, whilst healing deeply and profoundly.

The exercises in this workbook empower you to identify and transform the obstacles that distract you from the realisation of your unique purpose.

Dive into the flow of the 'wu- wei' where accomplishment feels easy, where every thought, feeling and action brings fulfilment and contentment.

This book is carefully crafted to provide a nurturing structure, within which you can explore, record and review your individual story,

Colouring pictures as you contemplate the content.

Choose a starting point that suits you and progress in your own way, be methodical, random or trust your inner guide.

Please be kind to yourself, whilst working with the exercises in this book.

Stop and take some time to colour when you need to.

Allow yourself to pause, reflect and breathe.

Think of this as a walk in a garden with a friend to confide in.

There are no correct answers.

Emotions, experiences or situations may surface that have a significant or lasting impact, permit yourself to acknowledge and release them, within the support of this nourishing space.

Helpful signposts along the way.

Each section contains exercises and opportunities for personal reflection, these are all bordered with a double line to make them easy to spot.
Feel free to colour the boxes, borders, lines and spaces or doodle wherever you wish, let your creativity flow.

The images are all monochrome line drawings, let your creativity flow as you travel through your story. Grab your colouring pens , feel free to colour, doodle and dream.

What this book is about

This book helps you identify you skills, talents, strengths and challenges and work with them to be the best version of yourself.

Helping you to preserve the precious and clear out anything holding you back.

Human beings are sophisticated pieces of organic engineering; running complex processes to keep us alive, effect running repairs and even build whole, new human beings.

Our world is very advanced with electric lights, cars and computers; but human beings still run our original programming, preoccupied with survival and continuation of the species, ensuring the best genes survive into the future.

Our programming responds to a world where savage beasts still regard us as tasty morsels and hunt us for food.

Whilst our bodies have adapted to changes in our physical environment, our autonomic systems still respond to threats with the same fight, flight or freeze responses, creating anxiety and preventing us from being the best version of ourselves.

If only our bodies had hazard warning lights to alert us to imminent malfunctions.

We rarely give our bodies the care and respect they deserve.

A daily wash and brush up, some food and sleep and the occasional trip to the dentist.

Beyond that, our complicated bodies only receive attention when something breaks or malfunctions, restricting our ability to function 'as normal'.

This book encourages the pursuit of balance and harmony with natural cycles, by accessing the energies constantly available around us.

The exercises are designed to improve personal insights and identify personal imbalances, whilst addressing any 'programming glitches' that may impair progress.

Use this book to have a personal de-frag and learn all about what makes you tick.

Examine your internal programming, identify the gaps, which bits are stuck, broken or malfunctioning and release whatever is past its best.

Use this book to discover the best version of you.

The five element cycle

When energy (Qi) flows harmoniously we perform gracefully, with ease.

In Traditional Chinese Medicine (TCM) this is known as being in the Wu-Wei (effortless achievement) and is the focus of many practices, including Tai Chi.

The 5 element cycle explores the relationships between the constituent parts of the cycle. Harmonising these elements achieves and maintains optimum flow of Qi, keeping us in the elegant flow of the wu-wei.

The 5 element cycle operates continually on all levels.
Every cell in your body experiences the cycle, on the largest scale, the universe is believed to be going through it too.

The five elements are most easily observed in the seasons in a temperate climate.
Each element also has an associated colour palette.

Wood	Spring time	planning, change and new growth	green colours
Fire	Summer time	high activity and significant achievement	red colours
Earth	Harvest time	gather in, reap the rewards of labour	yellow colours
Metal	Autumn time	preserve the precious, release what's done	white/grey colours
Water	Winter time	hibernate, reflect and dream in the next idea	blue colours

Momentum around the cycle is harmonised by two dynamic processes - Shen & Ko.
The shen cycle moves nourishing Qi clockwise around the five elements.
The shen cycle follows the circular flow of arrows on the diagram.

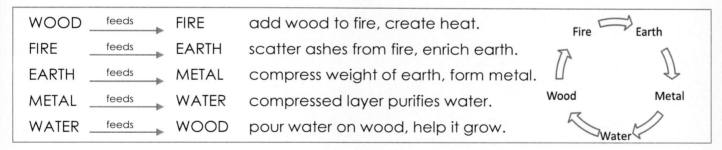

The ko cycle regulates the Qi flow by accelerating or reducing momentum.
The ko cycle follows the star shaped path of the arrows at the inside of the diagram.

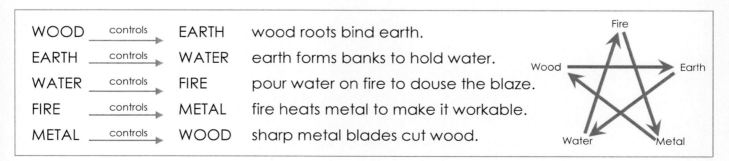

© Copyright 2020 clairecutlercasey.com

Meridians and how to work with them

Meridian pathways invisibly transport Qi and information around the system, to regulate body temperature and emotional flow, release water, co-ordinate and regulate various bodily functions and stimulate intrinsic healing mechanisms.

This book follows the flow of the five element cycle, starting from the Wood element in Spring. Each element contains at least two 'superficial' meridians.
The 12 'superficial' meridian pathways run bi-laterally around the body, creating a continuous circuit.

Wood element - Spring - contains Gall Bladder & Liver meridians.
Fire element - Summer - contains Heart, Small Intestine, Pericardium & Triple warmer meridians.
Earth element - Harvest - contains Stomach & Spleen meridians.
Metal element - Autumn - contains Lung & Large Intestine Meridians.
Water element - Winter - contains Kidney & Bladder meridians.

Central and governing meridians are separate from this cycle, creating a separate loop, running from the perineum to the head, up the front and back of the body.

Meridian energy can be worked through clothes, use a light pressure against, or just off, the surface of the body.

There are various ways to work with Qi through the meridian pathways.

Encourage harmony by working the meridian pathway on both sides of the body at any time of day, whenever you wish.

Try running a flat hand quickly or slowly along the meridian pathway, follow the direction of travel indicated on each diagram.

Holding or gently rubbing the end point of each meridian may also prove beneficial.
Try holding the start and end points on one side of the body and then the other.

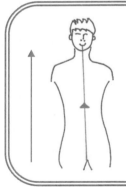

Up the front midline of the torso, running from the top centre of the pubic bone to the middle of the bottom lip.

The insights page, for each meridian, shows a picture of the meridian pathway and a brief narrative of the pathway and direction of travel.
Use this to explore each individual meridian pathway.

The meridians run in a continuous circuit in the following order through the day:

Stomach (07:00) → Spleen (09:00) → Heart (11:00) → Small Intestine (13:00) → Bladder (15:00) → Kidney (17:00) → Pericardium (19:00) → Triple warmer (21:00) → Gall Bladder (23:00) → Liver (01:00) → Lung (03:00) → Large intestine (05:00) →

To give your system a quick boost of Qi try running the meridians consecutively in this order, starting with the current time of the day.

The concept of yin and yang

It is impossible to change one thing in isolation.
Embracing the concept of yin and yang equips us to explore the impact of any changes we choose to effect.

Accepting change as the universal constant helps us each attain our own unique, harmonious still point.

The ancient philosophy of Yin and Yang explores the complex, elemental relationships between apparent opposites, how they co-create and co-exist dynamically, interdependent and inseparable, creating a mutual whole.

There can be no day without night, no heat without cold, no absence without presence; each always contains aspects of the other.

The concept of Yin and Yang explores the sophisticated dynamic within these relationships.

Yin and Yang each have tangible and abstract properties.

Some are set out in the table below, feel free to explore and add more of your own in the spaces provided.

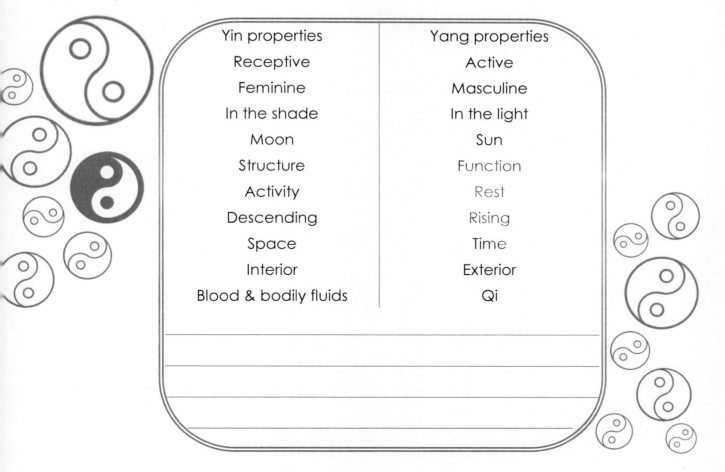

Yin properties	Yang properties
Receptive	Active
Feminine	Masculine
In the shade	In the light
Moon	Sun
Structure	Function
Activity	Rest
Descending	Rising
Space	Time
Interior	Exterior
Blood & bodily fluids	Qi

About the author and the birth of this project

In 2003 I was captivated by the concept of the Chinese 5 elements and have continued exploring it ever since.
Along the way I qualified as a professional kinesiology practitioner and instructor.
Studies into anatomy & physiology, psychology, nutrition and behavioural sciences further excited my interest in the complexity, sophistication and incredible capacity of human beings.

"Knowing yourself is the beginning of all wisdom"
Aristotle

In 2015 I devised a series of 12 'seasonal living' workshops. Sharing tips and techniques to help people live harmoniously with the cycle of energies, through the year.
In 2018 I further developed these to be delivered via Zoom, an online meeting platform.
This workbook evolved to create a space to explore and develop your story, at your pace, with the support of the energy surrounding us.

Working 1-2-1 with clients in my clinic, "The Happy Healing Hut", cemented my desire to create a workbook people could enjoy independently, at their own pace, either to support their work with me or to explore alone.

"Tell me and I forget, teach me and I remember, involve me and I learn"
Benjamin Franklin

At the time of writing I live and work on the edge of the Yorkshire Wolds.
Sharing my love of life with my pets.
We can often be found walking around the village together.

My modern day inspirations include Ken Cutler, Sir Terry Pratchett, Martin Luther King Jr, Sir Ken Robinson, John Thie and Courtney Pine.
For details of 1-2-1 clinic sessions, workshops, festivals and accredited training please visit www.clairecutlercasey.com

This project would not have been possible without the support of so many people.
I extend my sincere, heartfelt thanks to them all, and would especially like to mention:
Caroline Mott, Viv Chamberlin-Kidd, Tracey Johnson, Mel Statner, Penny Heater, Tricia Cable, Christine Uphill, Tracy Burleigh, Julie Elder, Dawn Emmerson, Lucy Monkman, Lucy Hart and George Tyson.

Central meridian insights

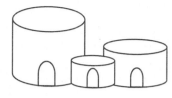
Central meridian is a storehouse of yin meridian energy; regulating and directing the yin meridian activity and storing spent yin energy, ready for release through exhalation.

Central meridian, also called conception vessel, is connected to all the yin meridians, it provides a release valve for excess and spent yin energy.

Central meridian energy is one of our ancestral meridians, forming a bridge between the energy we inherit from our parents and ancestors and the energy of our own personal energy flow, which flows through our superficial meridians.

What talents or beliefs have you inherited that require updating or releasing?	What talents did your ancestors have that you wish to embrace or reclaim?

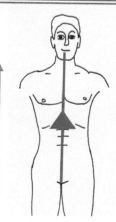

Central meridian energy runs up the front midline of the torso. Beginning at the pubic bone and terminating inside the bottom lip.

Try this: at times of shock, stress, tiredness or exasperation.
Run the palm of your flat hand up the front of your body, 3 times.
Start on the pubic bone and end on the bottom lip.
Do this any time you feel in need of balance and calm.

Use this page to record your thoughts and feelings. The words at the foot of the page describe emotions associated with the central meridian.

Curious Presence *Engagement* **Question** Enlighten Connect Clarity *Anchoring* **Success** *Perception* **Self-respect** **Wonder** **Overwhelm** Communicate *Expression* Shy Authenticity *Individuality* **Explore** *Vision* Unique

Releasing and updating to keep up with the times

Central meridian energy is future focussed, thrusting our heritage into the future, making it relevant for the next part of our journey and ensuring our lineage survives and thrives. Energy from the central meridian nourishes the uterus and reproductive organs, regulating the cycles of change, which occur every 7 years in women and 8 years in men.

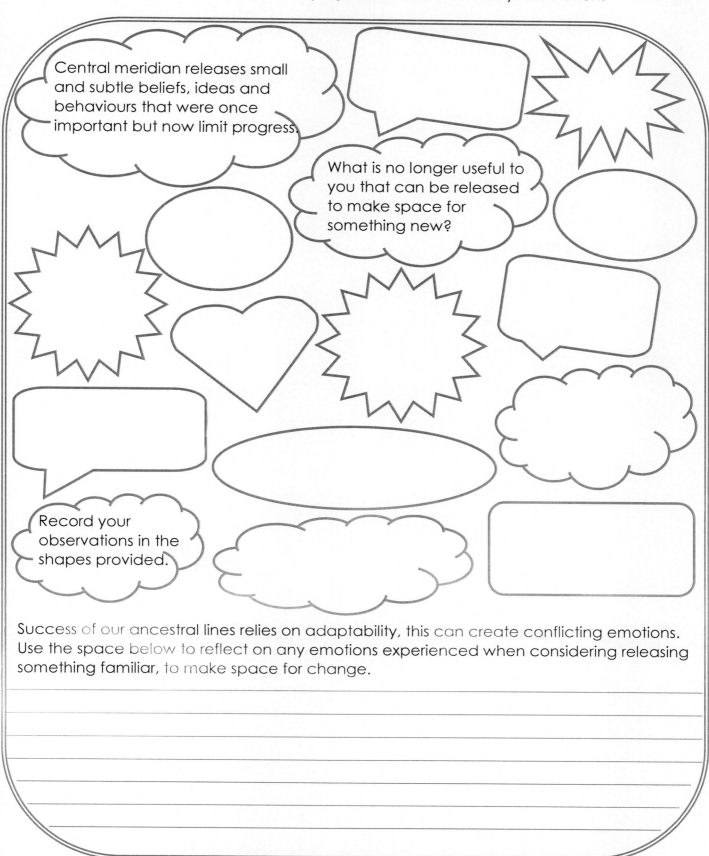

- Central meridian releases small and subtle beliefs, ideas and behaviours that were once important but now limit progress.
- What is no longer useful to you that can be released to make space for something new?
- Record your observations in the shapes provided.

Success of our ancestral lines relies on adaptability, this can create conflicting emotions. Use the space below to reflect on any emotions experienced when considering releasing something familiar, to make space for change.

Developing respect for intelligence

Your brain has learned to assess situations and make 'well-informed' guesses about what will work, based on previous outcomes.
Everything is viewed in retrospect.

Intelligence is a completely different system, combining past, present and future to explore what is actually happening, in the moment, and responding to it.
Intelligence observes situations as they unfold which is more efficient than guessing.

Using the past as a predictor of the future can be unreliable, clunky and outdated, leaving little room for innovation.
Creating a solution to a question that is no longer relevant.

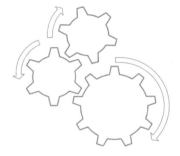

The temptation to 'fix' situations is a habit we learn as we mature.
Try letting go of this automatic response.
Create space and allow some magic to unfold.
Imagine leaving a situation to resolve itself without interference. How might that be?

_____
_____
_____
_____
_____
_____
_____
_____

Now try it. Choose a safe situation where you would usually jump in and 'sort it out'.
Resist the temptation, walk away, allow the situation to unfold.
Record your observations below.

_____
_____
_____
_____

Governing meridian insights

Governing meridian is the storehouse of yang meridian energy, regulating and directing the yang meridian activity and storing spent yang energy, ready for release through exhalation.
Governing meridian is known as the 'Sea of Yang meridians'.
It is responsible for the distribution of Guardian Qi to protect against external intrusion.
Guardian Qi is also called Wei Qi. Wei Qi circulates around the system in a monthly cycle, known as the flow of the Wu-Wei, where accomplishment feels easy.

Governing meridian is associated with brain activity and communication.
Harmonising governing meridian energy returns the music to the symphony of life.

Governing meridian imbalances suggest small burdens preventing easy transformation.
What small burdens weigh you down?

_____
_____
_____
_____
_____
_____
_____
_____
_____

Governing meridian energy runs up the back midline, following the path of the spine, over the head, down the midline of the forehead and nose, to the centre of the upper lip.
With the flat of your hand, run your hand along the length of the pathway, following the direction of flow.
Repeat 3 times whenever you feel in need of a boost.

Try this: when you need a tune up.
Gently press the tip off the tongue against the roof of the mouth.
Hold there for 5 long, slow breaths.

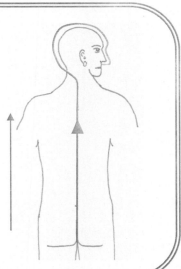

Use this page to record your thoughts and feelings. The words at the foot of the page describe emotions associated with the governing meridian.

Truth   Value   *Acceptance*   **Support**   **Honesty**   *Store*
Principle   *Dependence*   Assent   Pledge   *Belief*   **Fidelity**
Composure   Independence   Expectation   Trust   Reliance
Burden   **Commitment**   Honour   *Embarrassment*

Establishing core values

Defining a value set creates secure foundations for dreaming, planning, decision making and the continued pursuit of success.

Values are the basic behaviours and attitudes that underpin each individual, they are non-negotiable and do not require validation. It's ok to disagree regarding values.

Authenticity, confidence and surety come from reflecting on our own personal values, defining a unique set for ourselves and then living to them. Some may be fundamental, others may be more subtle.

Your values may emerge over time; it's worth reviewing your values periodically, as you work through the book.

The vocabulary of value words is vast, some are noted below.
Choose 12 value words that reflect your attitude, behaviour and ethos.
Record them in the boxes below. Tick the ones you consistently demonstrate.

1	2	3	4
5	6	7	8
9	10	11	12

How does it feel to have a defined value set? Record your thoughts below.

___

bohemian   elegant   structure   heroic   **HEARTFELT**   vital
spiritual   sophisticated   **practical**   fluent   dominating   exuberant
calm   bold   discerning   spirited   forthright   traditional   modest   easy
honest   quick   **fresh**   responsive   fierce   successful   warm   **bright**
inspirational   proactive   reliable   **flexible**   challenging   prudent
integrity   curious   gratitude   witty   **modern**   strong   reasonable
inclusive   tolerant   perfection   **accepting**   enthusiastic   brave
transparent   individual   **detached**   sustainable   creative
ambitious   eclectic   informed   innovative   compassion

Be wide awake or fast asleep

Are you tired through the day and wide awake at night?
Exposure to daylight and total darkness harmonises the pineal gland, regulating the sleep/wake cycle, improving sleep and enhancing mood.
Short winter days can impact the cycle, making it harder to stay awake during the day and to fall asleep at night.
Establish a daily routine and use some of the tips below to harmonise your body clock.

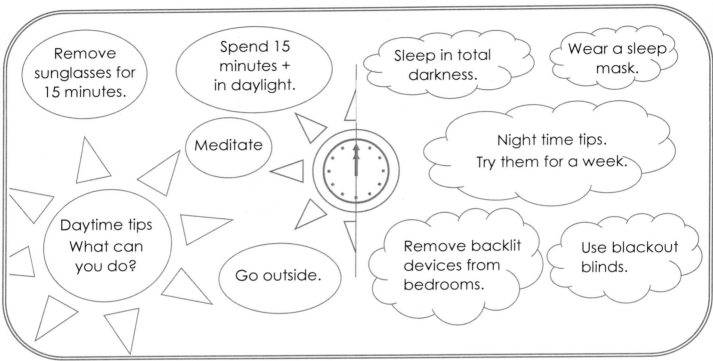

Posture affects how we interact, with ourselves and others.
Imbalances in Governing meridian energy may affect emotional or postural bearing.

Take a brief walk around, check in with your emotional and physical body.
Where is your centre of gravity? How flexible are your joints?
Make a note of how you feel in the following areas:

Knees	Rigid	Flexible
Hips	Rigid	Flexible
Shoulders	Stiff	Relaxed
Jaw	Clenched	Loose

Now work slowly up your body flexing, stretching, and rotating your muscles and joints.
Take another walk around, how are any aches, pains or imbalances?
Note the differences on the chart above and in the space below.

_____
_____
_____
_____
_____

Turn over a new leaf with wood element energy

Wood is nourished by water and feeds fire.
Wood drinks water through its roots.
Cut wood provides fuel for the fire.
Wood is controlled by metal and controls earth.
Metal is sharpened into blades to cut down wood, keeping it manageable.
The roots of wood bind the earth, holding it in place.
Too much wood can lead to indecision, preventing plans translating into action.
Too little wood can lead to sporadic activity, with unreliable results, lack of focus and daydreams that come to nought.
When the wood element is balanced we easily make choices and decisions
that fulfil our dreams and plans.
Experience smooth transition of thought into action, with balanced bursts of activity, punctuated by periods of rest.
Wood season is Spring, a time of new life and rapid change where energy pulses and rests.
Let the dreams of the future come into life with meticulous planning.
The meridians in the Wood element are Liver (Yin) and Gall Bladder (Yang).

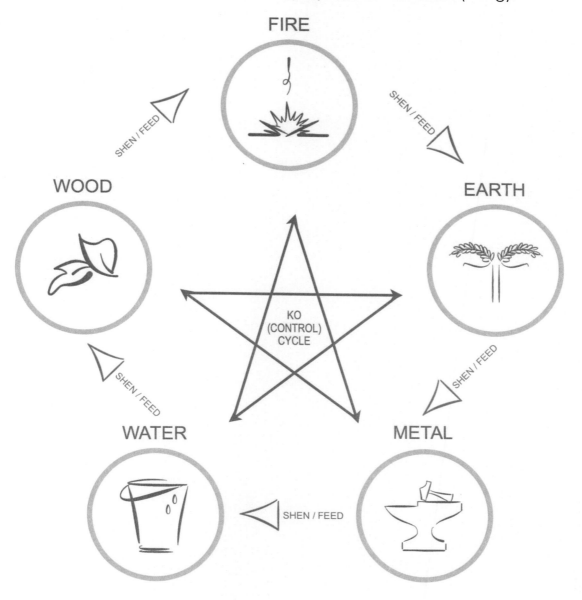

Use this page to record your thoughts and feelings. The words at the foot of the page describe various emotions associated with the wood element.

Humble **Indignant** Potent **Contentment** Boredom *Adore*
Resentment Decisive **Entitled** Hostility **Motivation**
Love Assertive *Choice* Anger *Transformation*
Pride **Bitterness** **Passive** Happiness *Rage*

Liver meridian insights

The liver is one of the hardest working organs in the human body, undertaking approximately 500 functions and supporting the function and good running of every other organ.

The liver is the only organ in the body that can re-generate itself, like your own internal time lord.

There is much to respect about liver meridian energy.

Liver is a recycling powerhouse.

Weighing approx. 1.5kg, it processes 3 pints of blood every minute.

Your liver detoxifies all the blood in your body more than 400 times every day.

The more 'stuff' you put in, the harder it works to get everything sorted, utilised and excreted.

Liver works to simultaneously secret biochemicals, including bile; supporting digestion, storing glycogen to maintain blood sugar levels, synthesising blood plasma proteins, decomposing spent red blood cells and breaking down toxins.

Liver meridian energy is most active between 1 am and 3 am.

When you're resting it's busy processing all the data from the day.

Use the tips at any time of day to support optimum liver meridian energy activity, whilst you sleep.

Liver meridian time is associated with personal growth and renewal.

Making spring a great time to clean up your act, mentally, emotionally and physically.

With the flat of your hand, trace the liver meridian pathway 3 times, starting on the foot.

Do this anytime you need reassurance during times of change.

The Liver meridian runs up both sides of the body.

Start on the inside edge of the big toe, trace across the inside top edge of the foot.

Continue up the inside leg to the groin. Back to the bottom of the rib cage and in towards the midline.

End halfway between the nipple and the bottom of the rib cage.

Dispelling the taboo of anger

When we are happy with the status quo we feel content.
Bitterness, irritability or resentment mean it is time to take responsibility and transform.
Liver meridian energy provides catalysts for change and power for transformation.

Anger creates the impetus for change, a thrusting force enabling transformation.
In the modern age anger is viewed as an emotion that needs to be supressed.
Expressing it safely, like other emotions, is an effective method of working through it.

Liver meridian energy maintains the healthy, harmonious flow of blood and Qi.
Attempts to hold back change creates energetic and emotional imbalances, which can lead to physical, emotional and mental health problems.
Learning to acknowledge, express and release anger can have a positive effect on all aspects of well-being.

Try this exercise to release anger without blame or judgement.

Choose a place where you are free to shout without impacting others.
Suitable locations could include a quiet road, a deserted windy beach or blustery hill.
If there are people around move as far away from them as possible and make sure there are no animals nearby.

Take a deep breath and shout clearly and loudly into the empty space
'I am angry at/about/because/that ………………………………………………………………………,'
Allow the energy of the moment to complete the sentence without thinking about it.
Take a breath, say 'Thank you'.
Take another deep breath and repeat until you feel spent.

Allow issues to emerge organically.
Some you may recognise, others may be surprising, acknowledge them and release them without getting caught up in blame, judgement or analysis.
Record your observations in the spaces below.

_____
_____
_____
_____
_____

How did you feel after this exercise? _____
_____
_____
_____

Spring clean your routine

Spring is a time for change, a chance to shake things up, get out of a rut and create new ways of being.

It's a time to renew the self as well as rejuvenating habits and ideas.

Liver meridian energy can be released it short bursts with some quick, simple changes.

- Get up 30 minutes early.
- Write a blog.
- Wear a hat.
- Get a project buddy.
- Draw a daily affirmation.
- Shop in a different store.
- Take up a new sport or hobby.
- Read a new genre of book.
- Sit in a different seat on the bus.
- Walk a different route to work.
- Visit a different museum.
- Take the kids to a different park.
- Try a new market.
- Join a sports team.
- Try a new recipe.
- Wear colour.
- Make a new workout playlist.

What small changes will you make? Record them below.

How many hats do you wear?

Difficulty focusing on one job at a time indicates liver meridian energy imbalance. Simultaneously attempting too many complicated tasks creates overload and burn out.

Liver meridian energy prompts us to be responsible, this includes taking responsibility for our own well-being.

When asked what we do, we choose the 'official' headline job title.

Often we juggle multiple roles and responsibilities, which require wrangling and management. Which roles are your responsibility or do you take responsibility for?

Write each role in a different hat in the space below.

Look at the roles above, which are the 5 most important?
Which roles can only be fulfilled by you?
Record them in the spaces below.

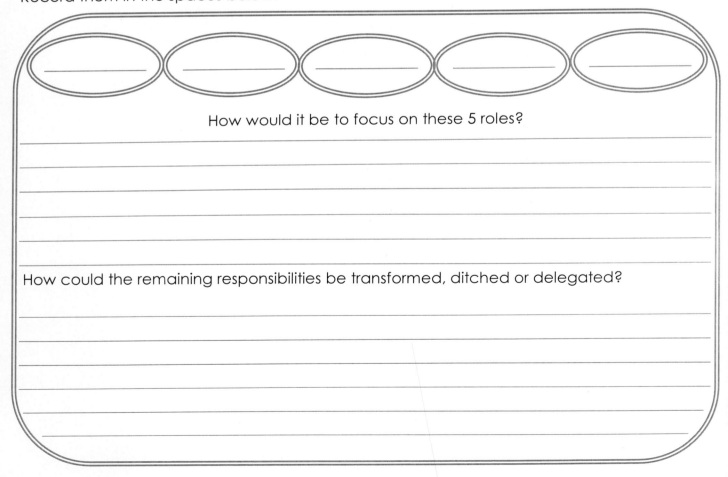

How would it be to focus on these 5 roles?

How could the remaining responsibilities be transformed, ditched or delegated?

Small steps to big changes

Change can feel daunting, exciting, inspiring and scary.
Some people crave change, whilst others actively avoid it.
Understanding our personal response to change ensures our ability to thrive in an ever changing world.

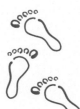

What words or images come to mind when you consider change?
_____

How do you feel when you contemplate change?
_____

Does your attitude depend on the perceived size of the change?
_____

Does your attitude alter if the change is your idea or someone else's idea?
_____

What happens physically when you contemplate change?
_____

Reflect on the answers above and sum up your personal response to change
_____

What does this mind set or feeling prompt you to do/prevent you from doing?
_____

If you could change one thing about yourself what would you choose and why?
_____

Take a chance → make a choice → change

Liver meridian energy is thrusting, powerful, assertive and transformative.
Make regular, deliberate choices to harness liver meridian power.
Transform your life, live deliberately, find freedom from unnecessary fear or guilt.
Whilst some habits save time, the cost to creativity can be high.
Routines can obstruct transformation, creating apathy and resentment.
Consider your response when the supermarket moves a product you regularly purchase.
Living deliberately shakes things up, building robust connections to your creative, assertive, decisive powerhouse within.

At the beginning of the week rate your creativity on a scale of 0-10.
0 = no creativity at all, 10 = super creative.
Use the chart below to shed some light on your habits, there's spaces for your own too.
Try changing at least one habit, each day, for a week.
Record your thoughts and observations.
At the end of the week rate your creativity again.

What routines do you have? Tick all that apply to you. Add your own in the spaces.		How can you shake things up? Try some of the examples and reflect on your experience. Add your own in the spaces.	
Take the same route.		New route.	
Do the same exercise.		Different lunch.	
Shop in the same store.		New store.	
Eat the same food.			
Drink the same drink.			
Wear the same shoes.			
Dress in the same outfit.			
Listen to the same artist/podcast/station/genre.			

What have you learned from this? Record your reflections below.

Find your happy

Happiness is the emotional state we talk about the most, either having it or wanting it.
In a comprehensive emotional vocabulary, happiness is the one state we crave.
Understanding what happiness means to us and where we find it provides valuable insights into what we're aiming to achieve and where to look for it.

Contentment is a sustainable state of being.
Pursuing contentment allows varying states of happiness to punctuate our lives, creating emotional wiggle room for an authentic experience of life.

Happiness comes in various forms, contentment, joy, ecstasy, pleasure, bliss.
Use the space below to explore what activities, beliefs or behaviours stimulate different types of happiness for you, and where you might find them.

What creates your *Contentment*

Where is your JOY

What nurtures your **Happiness**

When do you feel *Bliss*

What changes will help you experience these states regularly?

Thoughts

Actions

Ideas

Practical ways to support liver meridian energy

Beetroot is the secret ally of the liver.
It is full of anti-oxidants and glutamine and rich in betacyanin.
Add fresh beetroot to your diet.
Eating beetroot can turn urine purple so be prepared.

How is your eyesight?
Do your eyes feel tired, bright, sore, watery, clear, itchy?
Liver meridian is associated with eyes.
Give your eyes regular attention to help harmonise liver meridian energy.

Try this to exercise muscles around the eyes.
This exercise can invoke emotional release.
Sit or stand with your head straight on your neck, facing forwards.
Hold your head still.
Open your eyes and move them to look around each of the points on the clock face.
from 12 o'clock in a clockwise direction.
When you reach 12 o'clock again go back round the other way.
Close your eyes and repeat, keeping your head still at all times.
Rub hands together and place palms over closed eyes.
Take three long slow deep breaths.
Open eyes with palms over, then gently spread fingers before removing hands.

Liver meridian energy is the powerhouse of renewal.
To restore liver meridian energy reduce your caffeine, sugar and alcohol .
Intake. Replace them with pure, fresh water.
Add a slice of lemon/lime or a sprig of rosemary for flavour.

Try this to help improve focus and attention.
Go out for a walk, how many different things of one genre you can spot?
Look for : Flowers, birds, leaves, insects, trees, dogs, vehicles.
Don't worry about naming or recording them.
Spend time looking at each one and noticing the differences between them.

Detoxes support liver meridian energy and are better left until the first days of Spring, when the natural cleansing energies are best able to support and enhance your efforts.
Try starting your detox on the first day of Spring, feel the difference.

Gall bladder meridian insights

Gall bladder is the yang meridian of the wood element.
Also referred to as 'honourable minister', 'court of justice' and 'general's adviser'.

Gall bladder meridian energy governs daring and decision making.
The Chinese word for daring is 'da dan' meaning 'big gall'.
We say people have 'gall' when they take risks.
How could changing your attitude to risk help you?

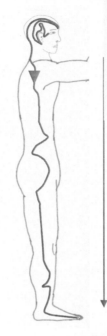

With the flat of your hand, trace the meridian pathway times on each side of the body, whenever you feel overwhelmed or want to improve decision making.

Gallbladder meridian runs on both sides of the body.
Begin on the outside corner of the eye, back to the ear, loop up, forward and around the temple, back behind the ear, up to the middle of the forehead, down behind the ear, behind the shoulder, behind the arm, down the side of the chest, hip and leg to the outside end of the fourth toe.

Gall Bladder secretes pure, potent bile, to digest and metabolise fats.
Fat is a very difficult substance to break down, bile acts like industrial detergent.
Gall Bladder meridian energy works with the lymphatic system to clear toxins from muscles, reducing muscle aches and pains.

Gall Bladder meridian energy provides the courage and initiative to transform kidney meridian ideas into fire element activity.

What's on your mind?
Keep a pen and paper handy, write down your thoughts to clear your mind and focus on the task in hand.

Gall Bladder Meridian energy is at it's zenith between 11pm and 1am.
Gall Bladder meridian energy influences quality and length of sleep.
Difficulty getting to sleep and trouble staying asleep can both indicate gall bladder meridian energy imbalance.
Use the tips before you go to bed, and through the day, to calm a racing mind, reduce overwhelm and promote restful sleep.

A bedtime story for grown ups

"Once upon a time, not so long ago, there was an exhausted grown up.
After a busy day they locked up the house and climbed into bed, ready for a restful sleep.
All was quiet, so the tired grown up switched off the light and snuggled under the covers.
Heavy with the need for sleep their eyelids drifted shut when, all of a sudden, BING!
A million thoughts began racing round their brain.
Mundane thoughts about locking up and feeding the pets soon made way for bigger issues, financial issues, strategic planning, world peace!
The tired grown up found themselves wide awake worrying about all sorts until, finally they gave up any idea of sleep, climbed out of bed, made a drink, worried about some of the stuff and switched on the TV……. "

For many this is a familiar bed time 'routine'.
Here's the good news.
This bed time activity is gall bladder meridian energy kicking in.
Gall bladder meridian energy breaks down difficult issues to create solutions.
Your busy day 'doing' hasn't made any time for 'thinking'.
When Gall Bladder meridian energy kicks in at 11pm it's ready to sort through your day, finding solutions while you sleep.

Try these simple hacks to get the most out of the penetrating force of gall bladder meridian energy.

Go to bed by 10:00 pm, aim to be asleep by 10:30 pm.

Set aside 'thinking time' each day.
Remove all distractions.
Allow thoughts to arise.
Ask yourself 'is this issue your responsibility?'
Do you have the power to change this?
If it's a feeling, place your hands where you experience it and breathe into it.
Acknowledge your thoughts and feelings.
It is not necessary to know the answer.

Keep a notebook and pen close by.
Record anything that keeps you awake.
What demands attention?
Do not engage with the thoughts.
Record them and return to sleep.

Starting at the toes, work slowly up your body tensing and releasing each limb in turn, breathing deeply as you go.

Motivation and where to find it

Motivation lives in gall bladder meridian energy.
It's the force that drives us to get something started.
It can be elusive so knowing where to find it and how to fire it up is a valuable asset.

Ideas forms in the Water element, sparking drive and vitality, passing the baton on to the ⟶

Wood element where courage, decision making, planning and impetus make the plan for action in ⟶

Fire element. Where passion, sustained activity and persistence bring the

If your motivation is lacking answer these questions honestly:

What are you working on?

Whose dream is it?

What do you have to lose?

What do you have to gain?

Do you believe in it?

If it's not your dream do you understand the vision?

What is the outcome going to achieve?

Create your own 'passion' for the outcome.
It might be getting paid, a day off, or the satisfaction of improving someone's lot.
Is the idea too risky or not risky enough?
If you have too much to lose/not enough to gain go back to the dream and re-negotiate.
Lack of belief in the outcome is demotivating and demoralising.
Take a step back, re-assess the idea, get a fresh perspective.
Is lack of belief justified? Make the outcome realistic.

Is your lack of belief unfounded? Change the internal narrative.
Try this:

Replace	*should*	with	*could*
Replace	*I can't*	with	*what happens if*
Replace	*won't/doesn't*	with	*might*

Paralysis by analysis and how to get out of it

When gall bladder meridian energy is out of balance we endlessly pick over situations.
All perspective is lost, the picture gets smaller and more intense.
The cycle gets caught up in itself and resolutions get further away.

Write down something you are undecided about here.
_____

Write one of your choices below.   Here write 3 positive outcome of that choice.
_____
_____
_____

Write another choice below.   Here write 3 positive outcomes of that choice.
_____
_____
_____

Write another choice below.   Here write 3 positive outcomes of that choice.
_____
_____
_____

Cover this column   Which of these outcomes do you prefer?
with your hand.   (Rate them from 1-9 if you like)

Exploring outcomes changes perspective.
Another way to do this is to explore what happens if you don't do something.
Try it here with one of your choices.
Does it make a difference to your preferred choice of action?

Write down something you are undecided about here.
_____

Consider here the consequences of doing nothing.
_____
_____
_____

Of ALL The options explored above, which appeals most?
_____
_____

Shift through the fog

Gall bladder meridian energy provides muscular strength and vitality.
Working with the lymphatic system, it clears toxins and reduces aches, pains and fatigue.
Unlike blood and oxygen, lymphatic fluid is moved round the body by physical exertion.
Try these hacks to free yourself from overwhelm, aches and the associated brain fog.

Walk away from the problem.
Get up and take a walk, use the stairs if you can.
Make physical space between you and the problem.
Move lymph out, draw clean, oxygenated blood in.
Return to it with a clear head, new insights and powerful solutions.

Tense shoulders and lift them as close to your ears as possible.
Breathe, slowly count to 3, then let your shoulders drop.
Feel the tension flood out as the release floods in.

Write down as many possible solutions to the situation as you can imagine.
Write each one on a separate piece of paper.
Fold each piece and place them all in a container.
On a separate piece of paper write "I am going to solve (name the situation) by…."
Pull one solution from the pot, at random, use it to complete the sentence above.
How does it feel?

_____
_____
_____
_____

Flipping a coin gives a clear indication of our feelings about each option.
Go with the option that feels best.

Imagine someone you admire and respect has come to you seeking advice about the same issue you are working on.
What advice would you give them?

_____
_____
_____
_____
_____

 The golden rule of decision making. If that decision doesn't work - make another.

Re-invent your life

It's very easy to get 'stuck in a rut', thankfully it's just as easy to get out.
Reinventing yourself is a great way to make changes.
Utilise the power of gall bladder meridian energy.
Asserting a different aspect of yourself changes your perspective on the world and your place in it.
Changes can be subtle or profound, large or small, the choice is yours.

"If you always do what you always did, you'll always get what you always got."
Henry Ford

- Is there a hobby you enjoy but haven't had time for? Get the equipment out and get stuck in.
- Do you have a hidden talent? Make use of it or offer it to someone else.
- Shake up your routine. Do mundane tasks on different days, visit a different class.
- If your meals are random, one pot, 'throw togethers', try following a recipe.
- Change your bag.
- Try a new hair style. Pull it forward, push it back, add a flower.
- What colours do you enjoy but seldom wear? Look at the back of the wardrobe, upcycle or wear them as they are.
- If life is a bit random add some structure.
- Re-jig your menu. Make new meals with your usual ingredients. Surf the net for ideas. Crack out the cookery books. Try something new.
- Shake up you wardrobe with a scarf, pair of shoes or socks. Visit charity shops.

Stepping stones out of overwhelm

Gall bladder meridian energy creates solutions from difficult issues.
Personal issues can feel over whelming, with too many considerations to be made.
Simplify the process by breaking it down.
Concentrate on one aspect at a time.

Try this: Consider your path as a series of stepping stones.
What individual steps can you take to get where you want to be?
Breaking the task down like this makes it effective and achievable.
Top Tip: Complete the final stepping Stone first.

Where are you starting from?
_____

What is the first thing you can do?
_____

What is the next thing you can do?
_____

What is the next action?
_____

What is the next action?
_____

Where are you aiming for?
_____

Everyday support for gall bladder meridian energy

Do something every day to stay motivated, maintain impetus and prevent overwhelm.
With gall bladder meridian energy small, regular changes create long term impact.

Everyday nutrition

Drink infusions. Try fresh ginger, lemon, fennel or peppermint.

Reduce caffeine intake.

Cut down alcohol consumption.

Remove sugary drinks and sodas.

Increase water intake.

Everyday changes create sustainable differences.

Feeling obliged creates resentment and hostility, creating an overwhelming sense of self-righteous indignation, using substantial energy with no outcome.

The task still needs doing.

Choosing to do a task releases the underlying tension.

The task gets done and energy is available to use elsewhere.

Try changing 'I have to' into 'I choose' for one week- feel the difference.

Record below any tasks you feel obliged to do, there's a couple of examples to start.

Laundry, walking the dog,

What thoughts and feelings are created by obligations?

Beside each 'have to' phrase below, record a task you do.

Record your thoughts and feelings about feeling obliged to undertake that task.

I 'have to'	Task	Feelings and thoughts experienced
I must		
I have to		
It's my job to		
I		

What thoughts and feelings are generated by choice?

Beside each 'choose to' phrase below, record the tasks from the table above.

Record your thoughts and feelings about choosing to undertake that task.

I 'choose to'	Task	Feelings and thoughts experienced
I choose to		
I want to		
I decide to		
I		

Spark up your fire, welcome joy & love into your life

Fire is nourished by wood and feeds earth.
Fire is stoked by putting wood on it.
The ashes from the fire add nutrients to the earth.
Fire is controlled by water and controls metal.
Water is used to douse the flames of fire.
Fire is used to smelt metal and make it workable.
Too much fire can be exhausting on the system, impacting periods of rest (water), depleting the later elements of earth (reward) and metal (letting go).
When the fire element is balanced we appreciate ourselves and others, we move ahead with our passions and recognise the outcomes of our efforts.
A balanced fire element eases the release what we no longer need.
Fire season is Summer, a time of long days and short nights, a season of heat and activity.
Keep hydrated (water) and rejoice in the joy of life (fire).
The meridians in the Fire element are Heart (Yin), Small Intestine (Yang), Triple Warmer (Yin) & Pericardium (Yang)

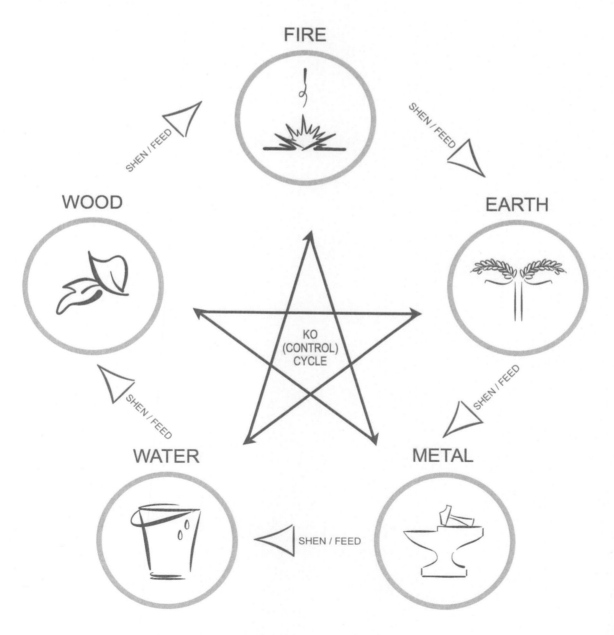

Use this page to record your thoughts and feelings. The words at the foot of the page describe some emotions associated with the fire element.

Remorse Worth Love Hope Buoyant Secure Responsible Calm Relax Excitement Shock Generous Passionate Active Forgiving Encouragement Balance Jealous Joy Desire Tranquil Lonely Appreciation Elation

Heart Meridian Insights

Heart meridian is the yin organ energy of the fire element.
Also referred to as 'king of the organs'.

Heart meridian energy is fundamental to our well-being and is well protected.
Physical protection is provided by the sternum (the bone at the centre of the rib cage) and the pericardial sac (see pericardium meridian).
Emotional protection is also provided by small intestine meridian energy.
The Chinese word 'hsin' refers to both heart and mind, affirming the connection between them.
Heart intelligence is more powerful than any other.
It has it's own receptors and electromagnetic force making it up to 70x more powerful than the most evolved part of the human brain.

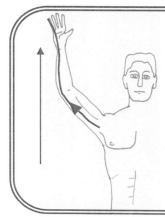

Heart meridian pathway runs on both sides of the body. Start from the armpit, continue up the inside of the arm and off the end of the little finger.

With the flat of your hand, start in the armpit and trace the meridian pathway 3 times, on each arm, to help re-centre into heart, reconnect with joy and calm down at times of stress.

Heart meridian energy is at it's zenith between 11am and 1pm.
Use these tips at any time of day to support heart meridian energy and enhance your connection with yourself and the world.
For a quick boost fling your arms out wide a few times or, better still, give someone a hug.

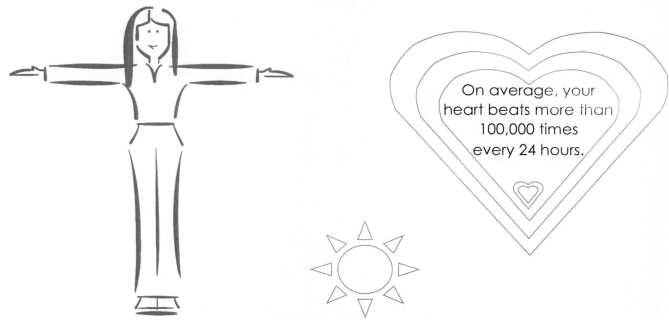

On average, your heart beats more than 100,000 times every 24 hours.

The heart pumps blood, oxygen and carbon dioxide around the body, under pressure.
In hot weather heart increases circulation to dissipate excess body heat.

Do you take things to heart?

The hearts' job is to efficiently transport oxygen and other nourishment to every cell of our being but, when we fail to engage with our own internal filters, we can end up taking on ideas, opinions, beliefs and behaviours that clog us up and weigh us down.

The sternum is the big bone that sits in front of the heart, protecting it from external physical injury; but what can we do to protect our heart from the words, emotions, beliefs and actions of others and ourselves?

Are you wounded by the words or actions of others?
Are you sensitive to criticisms, 'picking them over' or adopting them as part of your own internal narrative?

Combining directly with the discernment of the small intestine, we can learn to protect ourselves from the criticism, projection, anger and pain of others.

Try this to calm nerves.
- With palms facing you make a triangle resting thumb tips together and forefinger tips together.
- Rest this against your belly with the navel at the centre.
- Breathe deeply whilst focussing on this area.
- Imagine filling it with rich, golden light.
- Breathe steadily and feel the calm.

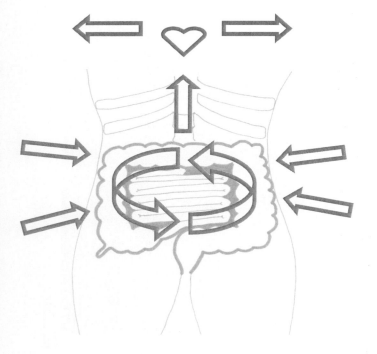

The belly houses the Solar Plexus.

Solar plexus aligns closely with small intestine energy and protects us from the fears, pains and insecurities of others as we listen.

Engage solar plexus by holding your hands over the area whilst listening, allow solar plexus and small intestine to filter out the essence of the message, communicating this to the heart, enabling a compassionate response.

On forgiveness

Forgiveness: *adj* a readiness to pardon, overlook, be merciful or compassionate.

Forgiveness means acceptance of fact and permission to move beyond it.
Forgiveness is how we acknowledge, witness and release the anger of injustice.
Forgiveness is not agreement.
The catharsis of forgiveness enables us to release anger and focus energy constructively.

Forgiveness is the attribute of the strong

Mahatma Gandhi

Forgiveness can reflect how an individual chooses to live their life.
Taking ownership of experiences and accomplishments remains with each individual, creating personal catharsis and healing.

Forgiveness is a journey, the milestones of which are honesty, courage, ownership and trust.
Take the first step using the questions below, there are no correct answers.
By acknowledging what we need we can work towards creating a forgiving space.
Go gently with yourself as you work through the process.

Consider a situation where you feel you have felt wronged.

Reflect on the following	Yes	No	What do you need & how can you get it?
Are you willing to forgive the situation and everyone involved?			
Are you willing to identify & release your emotions?			
Can you offer yourself compassion?			
Do you take full responsibility for your part in the situation?			
Are you willing to forgive completely?			
Do you trust the process?			
Do you trust yourself to release the pain and learn the lesson?			

What lessons has the experience taught you? _____

Fire up your passions

Engaging with the things we enjoy connects us with our passions, igniting fire energy, keeping the heart meridian happy and engaged.

Tasks flow and time passes quickly when we stimulate our passions.

Creating a life where passions are fuelled starts with identifying what drives us, only once the depths of our passions have been explored can we thrive; embracing the talents and skills that bring us alive.

Passion combines the love of a thing with a talent for it.

Place your loves and talents in the relevant spaces in the diagram, place any that fulfil both criteria in the intersection.

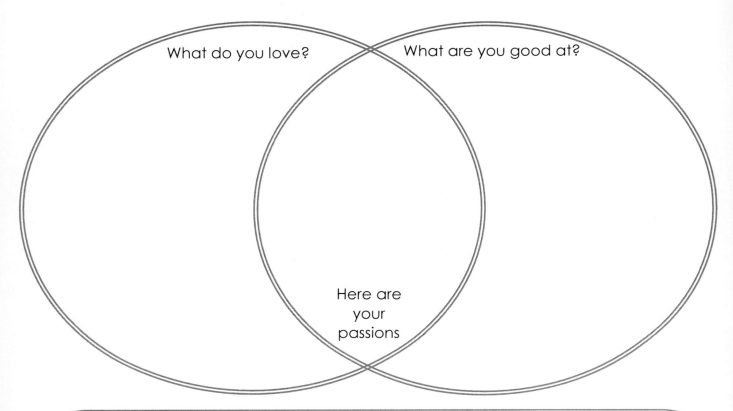

Reflect on your current life, are you making time for your passions?

If not, where could you find just 10 minutes, each day, to indulge your passions and keep your fire alive?

_____
_____
_____
_____
_____
_____
_____
_____

Joy is a potent emotion which nourishes and balances Heart meridian energy.
Help yourself connect easily with joy by recording everything that brings you joy.
Add more as you identify them.
Read your notes before going to sleep and on waking.

What are you grateful for today?

Expressing gratitude nourishes heart meridian energy.
Thank others, experiences and yourself.
Add things as you experience them.

Follow your heart

Following the heart is one of the simple steps of living in the wu-wei.

Seeking experiences that stimulate, strengthen and satisfy is what life is about.

Some suggest that working towards the hearts desire is selfish but, consider how different you are with others, when you feel fulfilled.

Isn't it more selfish to deny others that experience of you?

When we have spent a lifetime not following our hearts it, can feel a bit scary to start.

As soon as we decide to follow our heart, we get excited.

That's heart meridian energy doing a happy dance.

To follow your heart it's useful to know where your passions wish to take you.

Follow the process below to start some new conversations.

Record any observations, answers or emotions that arise in the spaces provided.

Step one: With both hands on your heart, breathe and listen. What do you hear or experience?

Step two: With both hands on your heart, ask yourself what you want. Breathe and allow the question to percolate, insights may take time.

Step three: With both hands on your heart acknowledge any emotions that arise, thank them and let them pass.

Step four: With both hands on your heart, ask what blocks you from following your heart. Breathe to allow insights and emotions to emerge.

Step five: With both hands on your heart, breathe and give yourself permission to follow your heart.

Never underestimate the power of the hug

Research demonstrates hugging is good for emotional and physical health.
Hugging stretches out these meridian pathways - check their chapters for more information on each.
A decent hug gives you, at least, 6 benefits in 1.

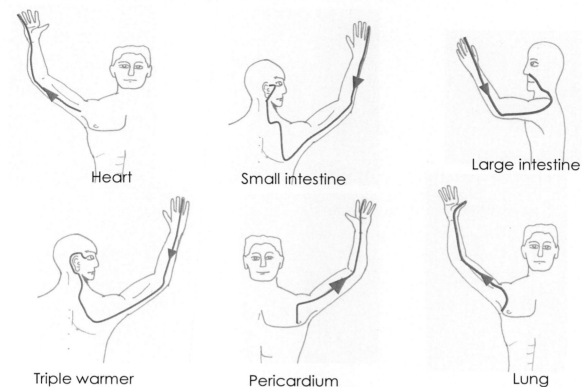

Heart — Small intestine — Large intestine

Triple warmer — Pericardium — Lung

The Good Hug Guide
Always ask permission, an unwanted hug is assault.
Stand with your feet at least hip width apart.
Keep feet flat on the floor.
Exhale to prepare.
Inhale to stretch arms out.
Exhale for the wrap around.
Inhale to begin the hug.
Relax into breathing and hugging.
Let breath calm & synch together.
Take a deep breath before disengaging.
Pull away gently.

Hugs lasting 20 seconds or more
→ calm breathing
→ increase release of feel good endorphins
→ raise oxytocin levels
→ balance the central nervous system

Stoke your fire with a riot of colour

Enjoyment of food starts with the eyes.

Summer is the perfect time to create a riot of colour on your plate.

Stimulate all your senses and bring joy and excitement to heart meridian energy.

Food made with love tastes completely different to anything mass produced, if it's home grown then the taste is even better.

> Try growing herbs, mustard and cress, edible flowers, cherry tomatoes or salad leaves indoors, if you don't have any outside space.
>
> The smallest outdoor space can be used for growing.
>
> Get a tub and grow. What will you try?
>
> _____
> _____
> _____
> _____
> _____
> _____
> _____
> _____
> _____
> _____

Mint, thyme, oregano, rosemary, chives and sage grow easily in most gardens.
Once planted they provide fresh, full flavours for years to come.

Investigate local veg sales, gardening clubs and village markets.
Allotment holders often sell off their surplus, you might even be tempted to get involved.

Fresh fruit & vegetables are full of flavour, packed with vitamins and minerals, fibre, water and natural sugars, most can be eaten raw and are great for snacking on too.
A summer diet containing fresh veg and fruit helps keep the whole system in peak emotional and physical condition.

Pericardium Meridian Insights

The Pericardium meridian is the yang fire organ energy meridian.

Also known as 'circulation sex', 'heart protector', 'guardian of the heart' and 'king's bodyguard'.

The pericardium is a durable, double walled membrane sac around the heart, anchoring the heart in place, regulating heart rhythm and protecting the heart from physical injury and infection.

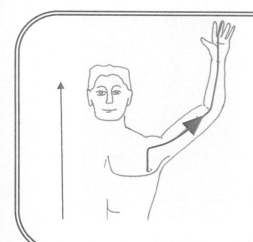

The meridian pathway runs on both sides of the body. Start at the nipple, move up to the front of the shoulder, down the middle of the inside of the arm, to the end of the thumb side of the middle finger.

With a flat hand, trace the meridian pathway 3 times on each side, this strengthens and balances pericardium meridian energy, reducing the impact of emotions when they run 'out of control'.

Pericardium Meridian Energy is at it's height between 7 pm and 9 pm but you can use these tips at any time to help you feel joyful, embrace the pleasure in life and get back on top of your game.

Pericardium meridian energy protects heart meridian energy from damage or disruption, caused by excessive emotional energies (Qi) and radical fluctuations knows as 'the excess of the 7 emotions'

These excesses make it difficult to utilise Qi, disrupting ease of movement around the system, impairing optimal performance.

Pericardium meridian energy protects and stabilises the heart meridian energy against the impact of the following excesses.

1. Too much **anger** makes Qi rise, **impairing the ability to ground**.
2. Too much **joy** makes Qi relax, **reducing activity**.
3. Too much **sadness dissipates Qi** making it difficult to muster.
4. Too much **fear** causes Qi to descend, **impacting aspiration**.
5. Excess of **temperature** affects Qi in different ways:
    When we are **too cold** Qi collects **impacting dexterity and clarity**.
    When we are **too hot** Qi moves out **impacting focus**.
6. Excess **fright** throws Qi into chaos **impairing the ability to gather our self together**.
7. **Exhaustion** wastes Qi leading to **further exhaustion and trouble functioning**.

Power, strength and subtle energy

Balanced Pericardium meridian energy supports emotional strength, enabling us to act clearly, resolutely and productively in challenging situations.

Working with pericardium meridian energy promotes objectivity; assisting us to observe the situation rather than getting sucked into the emotional vortex.

Pericardium meridian energy provides the strength to remain centred during times of stress, the power to move through traumatic situations, healing emotional wounds, whilst remaining solution focussed.

Under stress breathing gets shallow and fast, speech quickens and the vocal cords tighten, making the voice higher.

The brain identifies the higher voice as panic, creating a self-perpetuating cycle.

Break the cycle, try this:

In challenging situations focus on slowing your breath by breathing out completely, then pausing briefly, before taking another inhale.

Learn to control your speech by practicing speaking very slowly, when relaxed. Take regular pauses and breathe between sentences.

Deepen the tone of your voice by aiming low and speaking from the belly.

Observe the impact this has on yourself, other people and the situation.

Yourself	Others	Situation

Record your thoughts on this exercise here:

Preserving the gifts and mysteries

Pericardium meridian energy holds the balance of what is shared and what is private. Privacy may feel endangered in a time of 24/7 news and the social media appetite for life stories, but it's easier to manage than a hasty over-share.

What aspects of yourself, your life or your story do you prefer to keep private?

Pericardium meridian energy protects what is precious, ensuring it can be passed on to the next generation, creating a legacy for the future.

What wisdom was gifted to you?

What will you preserve and gift to the next generation?

Updating the legacy

Working with Pericardium provides an opportunity to update the wisdom and legacy, before passing it forward.

The gift can be to the next generation, or even the next phase of life.

What needs to be different to ensure improved outcomes?

Consider what changes would enhance your legacy going forward.

Can any restrictions be removed?

Are there beliefs that need updating or behaviours that no longer serve?

Dare to dream, defy convention!

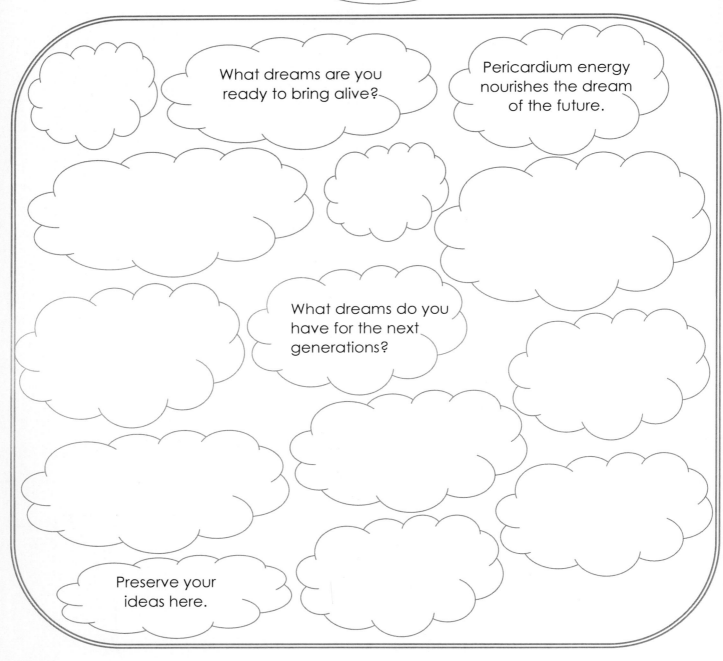

What dreams are you ready to bring alive?

Pericardium energy nourishes the dream of the future.

What dreams do you have for the next generations?

Preserve your ideas here.

Seek silence, speak softly

Hearts are valuable, vulnerable pieces of kit, without which we cannot function.
Your body has inbuilt physical and emotional protection.
The sternum protects the heart from external physical attack and the pericardium guards emotional and physical resilience.

Silence is a source of great strength
Lao Tzu

Silence and patience benefit pericardium.
Trends of over sharing create a constant pressure to maintain a stimulating narrative.
Focusing on silence and patience develops personal integrity, supports personal boundaries, protects what is most valuable and deepens mystery.
Try some of these tips to cultivate comfort and peace in silence and find your still point.

Observe without comment.
Take a journey without music or radio.
Switch off all distractions.
Take a walk without devices.
Journal your thoughts.
Swim.
Meditate.
Try origami.
After any activity sit in silence for a few minutes.
Yoga.
Tai Chi.
Breathe.

Use this space to journal your own thoughts on silence.

Your vibe attracts your tribe

Pericardium meridian energy forms part of our internal bonding process, pulsating the vibe that attracts our tribe.

Strength is vital to pericardium.

Consider carefully what energy you are projecting out into the world, think of your emotions like beacons shining out, seeking similar vibrations to connect with.

What thoughts, beliefs, emotions and values do you pulse out into the world?
_____
_____
_____
_____

Fill the rays of the beacon with the vibes you'd like to attract, do they match the ones in the table above?

What are you projecting?

Give yourself permission to live

Release the internal tension of self-denial and shame.
Support pericardium, seek happiness.
Give yourself permission to do what you enjoy & enjoy what you do.
Complete the slips below to remind yourself.

Pericardium Permission slip

I (insert name here) ....……... give myself permission

to enjoy (insert activity here)..

On (insert date)..

Pericardium Permission slip

I (insert name here) ....……... give myself permission

to enjoy (insert activity here)..

On (insert date)..

Pericardium Permission slip

I (insert name here) ....……... give myself permission

to enjoy (insert activity here)..

On (insert date)..

Pericardium Permission slip

I (insert name here) ....……... give myself permission

to enjoy (insert activity here)..

On (insert date)..

Pericardium Permission slip

I (insert name here) ....……... give myself permission

to enjoy (insert activity here)..

On (insert date)..

Heaven scent

Scent is a powerful balancer for pericardium meridian energy.
Adding scent to your everyday routines has many beneficial effects.
Add fragrance to warm the inner fire of pericardium meridian energy.
Take a moment to stop and smell the roses or adopt a more considered approach, use essential oils and specifically selected scents.

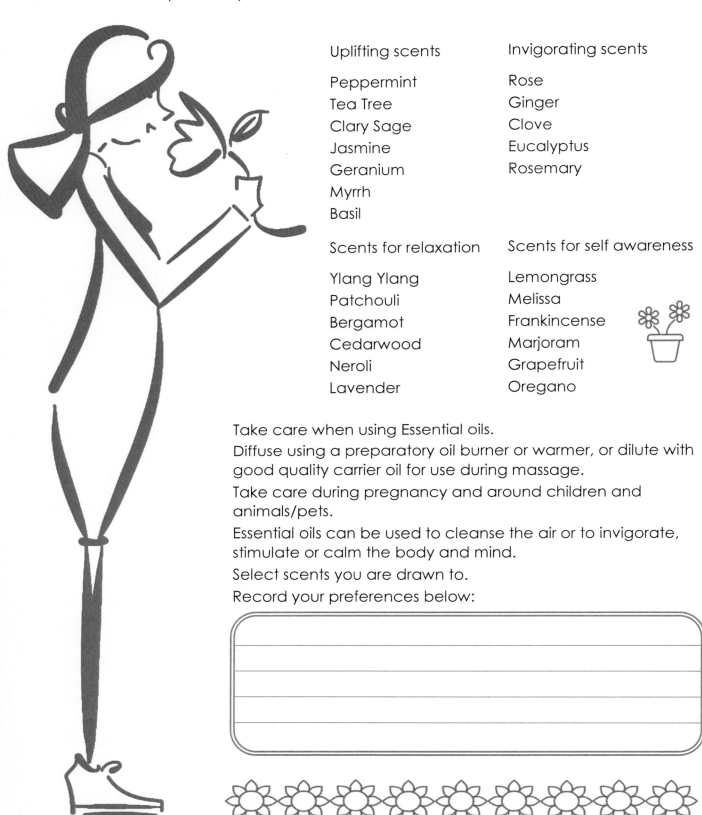

Uplifting scents

Peppermint
Tea Tree
Clary Sage
Jasmine
Geranium
Myrrh
Basil

Invigorating scents

Rose
Ginger
Clove
Eucalyptus
Rosemary

Scents for relaxation

Ylang Ylang
Patchouli
Bergamot
Cedarwood
Neroli
Lavender

Scents for self awareness

Lemongrass
Melissa
Frankincense
Marjoram
Grapefruit
Oregano

Take care when using Essential oils.
Diffuse using a preparatory oil burner or warmer, or dilute with good quality carrier oil for use during massage.
Take care during pregnancy and around children and animals/pets.
Essential oils can be used to cleanse the air or to invigorate, stimulate or calm the body and mind.
Select scents you are drawn to.
Record your preferences below:

Small intestine meridian insights

Small intestine is the yang organ energy of the fire element.
It is also known as the 'minister of reception'.

The Chinese term 'duan chang' means 'broken intestines' and equates to the western term 'broken heart', illustrating the close relationship between small intestine and heart meridian energies.

Small intestine meridian energy is responsible for separating 'the pure from the impure' and supports the emotional resilience of the heart meridian energy by creating clarity.

On both sides, begin on the outside end of the little finger, run along the outside of the arm to the base of the shoulder blade, continue up to the neck, across the cheek towards the nose and then back to the front of the ear.

With the flat of your hand, start on the outside end of the little finger of the opposite hand, slowly and gently trace the meridian pathway 3 times on each side.
Great for getting back on track after a big lunch or any time of day.

When your brain feels foggy stand up, stretch both arms up, out and back whilst breathing deeply, repeat 3 times, feel clarity return.

Small Intestine Meridian energy is at its height between 1pm and 3 pm, no coincidence that this is when we eat and digest lunch.
Use the tips in this section at any time to help improve discernment and restore clarity.

Adult small intestine is approximately 7m long, all packed into your abdomen.
Try sitting up straight to make some space.

Develop your internal discernment

Small intestine is vital in survival, extracting nourishment from everything ingested and supporting the continual fight against infection.

One of the first organs to form in the womb, small intestine connects directly to the mother through the umbilicus.

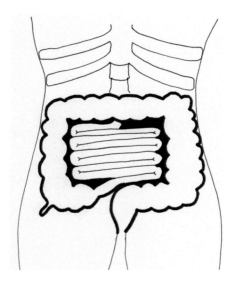

In an adult the small intestine is 6-7m long with a diameter of 2.5 cms and an absorption area of 30m^{sq}.

Areas in the wall of the small intestine, called Peyer's Patches, sample unrecognised substances, working closely with the immune system, to identify and defeat unwelcome invaders.

Working like a change sorter, small intestine extracts the constituent parts from everything you ingest, efficiently exchanging them into the blood stream, for instant transportation and delivery around your body.

Small intestine ingests emotional nutrition, beliefs and criticism in exactly the same way; everything takes this incredible journey of nourishment, so making choices about what we take on board is a short cut to joy.

Work with small intestine meridian energy to protect against damaging thoughts, ideas and beliefs and develop your emotional immunity.

Every day you carefully select clothes, shoes and a nourishing breakfast.
Choosing what criticisms, ideas and beliefs you take on board is a habit worth cultivating, to keep your emotional body healthy.

What do you take on board that doesn't nourish you?

_____
_____
_____
_____
_____
_____

How does this awareness affect your attitude to what you ingest?

_____
_____
_____
_____
_____

Digging for buried treasure

Small intestine meridian energy sorts out the gold from the gravel.
The 'gold' is anything that nourishes the physical, emotional and energetic self.

Food is an obvious source of nourishment so a balanced diet helps.
Sometimes the hunger is not for food, but for something else.
It's enlightening to discover what that is; try this exercise.
There's a completed example first to help.

> I love feeling <u>the sand under my feet</u>. When I <u>walk on the beach</u> I feel <u>free and alive</u>. Making time to do that is <u>always a consideration</u> on my priority list, because <u>I know how much better I feel when I do it</u>. The last time I took time out to <u>go to the beach</u> was <u>two weeks ago</u>, that feels <u>nice.</u>

Try filling in the 'story' below to find your own hidden treasure

> I love feeling _____.
> When I _____ I feel _____.
> Making time to do that is _____ on my priority list, because I _____.
> The last time I took time out to _____ was _____ ago, that feels _____ .

Dig deeper for more treasure.
Identifying emotional responses to situations is a great step on your self-awareness journey.
Use the table below to explore, there's a completed example to start you off.

When I	*make time to read*	I feel	*relaxed and contented.*
When I		I feel	
When I		I feel	
When I		I feel	
When I		I feel	
When I		I feel	
When I		I feel	
When I		I feel	
When I		I feel	

To do or not to do, that is the question

Using task lists can be empowering, clearing your mind to focus on the task in hand.
Task lists only work if the motivation is right.
Raise your game with this upgraded take on 'to do' lists.

Before starting a 'to do' list, consider why you are doing these tasks.
Who do you want to be? Where do you want to get? What's the end result?
Transform your 'to do' list into a 'to be' list and it's easy to get the right stuff done.

- Who do you want to be?
- What is the end result?
- How long will you take?
- Where are you headed?

Record your thoughts in the space below. Use an extra sheet if required.

Once you've worked out the who, what, when and where, it's time to start on the 'how'.
Work out how much time is available, each day, to allocate to your tasks.
Planning to fit too much in to the available time is demoralising; defeating motivation.
Use the 24 hour planner on the next page.
Make 7 copies and complete 1 for each day where your commitments differ.
First block out the times you're already committed to other set tasks such as
Sleeping, School run, Work, Sports Classes, Dog walks etc.
Be honest.
How long do these tasks really take?

_____day

Time	Task	Time	Task
05:00		17:00	
05:30		17:30	
06:00		18:00	
06:30		18:30	
07:00		19:00	
07:30		19:30	
08:00		20:00	
08:30		20:30	
09:00		21:00	
09:30		21:30	
10:00		22:00	
10:30		22:30	
11:00		23:00	
11:30		23:30	
12:00		00:00	
12:30		00:30	
13:00		01:00	
13:30		01:30	
14:00		02:00	
14:30		02:30	
15:00		03:00	
15:30		03:30	
16:00		04:00	
16:30		04:30	

Knowing how much time is available, in the day, helps prioritise time to devote to achieving the tasks that improve your situation.

Use this space to remind yourself who, where or what you want to be.

Work with small intestine energy - Let's do this

When you take on a new project or challenge it's easy to get swamped quickly, taking on too much and burning out.

Use the power of small intestine meridian energy to break your challenge into digestible pieces and get further in the time available.

Use the next page to break your tasks down into individual actions.

Use the tips here to get them done in the time available.

Top Tips for spending your precious time on valuable tasks that get you where you want to be.

Set time aside in your diary/planner and write the task(s) you will achieve in this time.

Be realistic.

Learn to say 'No' and stick to it.

Delegate

Remind yourself why you are doing this - what do you want to be different in your life?

Write completed tasks on slips of paper and store in a jar, feel the accomplishment as it fills.

Allocate EACH task a set time.
When the time is up move on to the next task on your schedule.
Be disciplined.

Aim for achievement, not perfection.

Set aside some time to nourish yourself.

Keep a completed list. Reflect on this when motivation is low.

Respect your efforts & acknowledge your achievements.

Avoid multi-tasking. Focus on one task at a time.

Use tips from small intestine insights page.

Ask for help.

Plan in time for social media, magazine reading, calling friends etc.

Avoid unscheduled interruptions to your day.

Be Ruthless - Prioritise tasks with this simple rating system.
- A = Important & close to deadline - do first.
- B = Important, no deadline, brings completion of outcome closer - do second.
- C = Nice to do - make some time for yourself each day, if only 5 minutes.
- D = Doesn't help get you where you want to be - ditch or delegate.
- E = What is this doing on your list? It's nothing to do with you! Erase.

Use this space to break down your challenge into individual tasks.
Don't worry about the order, that can be sorted once your task list takes shape.
Use this space to collect every job involved.
The example may give you some ideas.

Goal: Write a book
- collate ideas
choose favourite
- research themes
organise themes
- sketch out time line
- how many pages?
organise layout
- buy paper and ink
- source illustrator
- source technical editor
- source proof reader
- source testers
create test process
collect feedback
analyse feedback
- source printer
research prices
agree timeframes
- find finance
- marketing
social media
word of mouth
book signings
events
- write
- edit
- research
- choose title

Prioritise action

Imagine you have to eat a life sized chocolate elephant.

It's tempting to shove in as much as you can, but quickly you'd get sick of chocolate and, in no time, the thought of eating another piece feels horrible.

Soon you're doing anything else to avoid eating the elephant.

Eating your elephant one small bite at a time makes the impossible possible and keeps you coming back for more.

> Try this: Put a time against every job on your task list.
> If a single task will take more than 60 minutes see if you can break it down further.
> Shorter tasks are easier to achieve.

Let's prioritise.

Prioritisation enables you to complete tasks in an efficient flow making the most efficient use of the limited time and resources available.

> Try this simple exercise to practice.
> Task: Make a gin an tonic.
> Put these steps in the best order to make a gin and tonic.
>
> | Pour gin | Make ice | Enjoy | Get glass | Slice lime | Find knife | Pour tonic |
> |----------|----------|-------|-----------|------------|------------|------------|
> | | | | | | | |

Use all the information on this and the previous 4 pages to work out your plan.

Put your tasks in order of priority, and write them into the time spaces available on your daily schedules.

If you have 30 minutes each day by the end of week 1 you will have completed at least 7 tasks/3.5 hours towards your goal.

Reflect on your feelings and observations on this process.

_____
_____
_____
_____
_____
_____
_____

Triple warmer meridian insights

Triple warmer is the yang meridian of the fire element organ energy meridians.
Also known as the 'triple heater', 'minister of dykes and dredges' and the 'official of balance and harmony'.
Triple warmer meridian energy relates to a functional energy system that regulates the activity of the other organs, responsible for producing and circulating nourishing and protective energies.

Upper burner is located in chest controls intake

Middle burner is in the upper abdomen controls transformation

Lower burner in the lower abdomen controls elimination

Triple warmer meridian energy is where 'old habits die hard'.
Whatever the habit, behaviour or addiction triple warmer is the meridian energy that keeps it alive.
Working to balance and calm triple warmer meridian energy can support resolution of old habits that hold you back and prevent transformation.
Triple warmer meridian energy is at it's peak between 9 pm and 11pm.
Use these tips at any time of day to fuel your passions and ditch old habits.

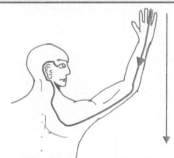

On both sides of the body,
start at the end of the ring finger,
up the back of the hand and arm,
across shoulder blade,
up the side of the neck,
behind the ear to the outside corner of the eye.

With the flat of your hand trace the meridian pathway 3 times on each side of the body to balance disproportionate emotions.

Whenever cravings or hot flushes hit, calm your system and ease your transformation by tracing the meridian pathway, in the opposite direction, 3 times on each side, with the flat of your hand.

Break the habit

Triple warmer meridian energy adapts to changes in circumstances, compensating for sleep deprivation, poor hydration, caffeine use, even addictions.

Triple warmer meridian energy develops and maintains coping mechanisms, sustaining us against potentially damaging, habitual behaviours.

When we are our own worst enemy, triple warmer meridian energy can be our best ally.

When we decide to clean up our act, sleep better, cut down caffeine, alcohol or drugs, triple warmer meridian energy can feel vulnerable, rewarding us with sweats, tremors, clouded thinking, loose bowels, disrupted sleep and obsessive thought patterns.

Dramatic life changes can create chaos in sensitive bodily systems, as they struggle to find a new equilibrium.

With foresight and persistence we can re-educate triple warmer meridian energy's obsessive behaviours, dump the addictive, destructive behaviours and emerge like the phoenix from the flames.

Try this:
Run triple warmer meridian pathway backwards.
Start at the corner of the eye, trace back,
around the top of the ear,
down the neck,
across the shoulder blade
down the outside of the arm and
off the end of the ring finger.
Repeat several times on each side of the body.
Thank the meridian energy for it's work as you go.

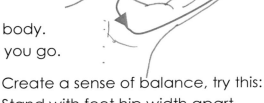

Create a sense of balance, try this:
Stand with feet hip width apart.
Lift right foot off the ground.
Balance on the left.
Breathe.
Count to 10.
Transfer the weight to the left foot.
Lift the right foot.
Breathe.
Count to 10.
Repeat 3 times.

To calm the panic try this:
Encircle the ring finger of the left hand with the four fingers of the right hand.
Rest the right thumb in the palm of the left hand.
Rest both hands in lap, close eyes and breathe.
After a few minutes swap.
Encircle the ring finger of the right hand with the four fingers of the left hand.
Rest the left thumb in the right palm,
Rest both hands in lap, close your eyes and breathe.

Good fences make great neighbours

Boundaries are crucial to good relationships, with ourselves and others.
Boundaries create firm foundations of expectations and respect, allowing growth.
Whilst boundaries may be negotiable, they let everyone know where they stand.

Imagine you need something from a shop with no set trading hours.
How does that feel? How would you go about getting what you need?

_____
_____
_____

Consider your boundaries. Which statement below best describes them?

I don't need boundaries, I'm a natural giver.	I like to fool myself by thinking I have boundaries.	I have different boundaries, with different people, on different days.	My boundaries are fixed, there's a little bit of flexibility, if I choose.	My boundaries have guards posted at every tower. No room for manoeuvre.

By setting boundaries we create a defined space with clear rules.
Ownership of communicating and maintaining the rules is ours alone.
Boundaries create a clear dynamic, helping everyone to get their needs met.
What needs do you have that are not being met? Record your thoughts below.

_____
_____
_____
_____
_____

What can you do differently to help you meet these needs?
Are you meeting the needs of others at the expense of your own?

_____
_____
_____
_____
_____

What rules or boundaries do you need to put in place and with whom?

_____
_____
_____
_____

Communicating and maintaining boundaries

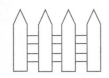

Deciding on the rules, limits and boundaries needed is the first step.
Getting others on board, to respect and work within them, requires effort.
Follow these ground rules for successful boundaries.

1. Be consistent.   Set a boundary or rule and stick to it. Consistency creates clarity.
2. Be fair.   Treat all equally. Respect others boundaries.
3. Be Patient.   If boundaries are new others may take time to adapt.
4. Be congruent.   If the boundary creates time for you make sure you use it.
5. Be positive.   Positive rules and boundaries are easier to assert and follow.
6. Be grateful   Demonstrate gratitude when boundaries are respected.

Boundaries can feel significant, if people have not previously experienced them.
Ease implementation with a little skill and judgement.
Always say 'thank you' when someone respects a boundary, gratitude is reward in itself.
When setting and re-stating the boundary, repeat exactly what you said previously.
Clear, calm, consistent messages are easier to understand and remember.

Get buy in from others affected, ask for their ideas.

Offer a skill swap. "You wash up, I'll mend your trousers."

Ignore deflections or diversions. Stay on message.

When negotiating focus on a 'win : win' resolution, where both parties feel heard.
Avoid personal comments, negotiate with the other person about the issue.
Remember why the boundary was created, ask the other person for their solutions.
Learn to say 'No', without qualification.

Practice saying 'No'.
Say 'No' and then stop talking.
Record your observations and reflections here.

_____
_____
_____
_____
_____
_____
_____

Benefits of meditation and breath work

When triple warmer meridian energy is out of balance it can be an emotional rollercoaster, bouncing chaotically between hope, despondency, loneliness and elation, using precious energy creating heightened emotions, with no results.

Making space, each day, for simple meditation and breath work focuses this energy on creating tangible results towards the next outcome.

What breath work or meditation techniques do you already use and how often?

Meditation enhances conscious awareness by developing inner understanding.
Try a walking meditation to create active relaxation for body and mind.
Other active meditative practices include T'ai Chi, Yoga, colouring and Chi Gung (Qigong)

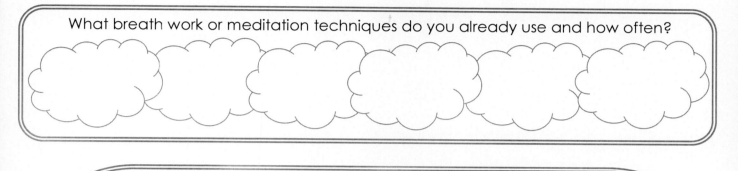

Try this:
Wear flat shoes or go barefoot, if conditions allow.
Find a safe, even, outdoor space to walk steadily, without obstruction.
Adopt a comfortable, flexible, upright posture.
Allow joints to move flexibly.
Allow opposite arms and legs to move together, fingers relaxed, palms open.
Breathe comfortably and rhythmically.
Direct your attention to the movement of your body.
Take slow, rhythmic deliberate steps.
Observe the sensations in your body as you move.
Identify areas of tension or discomfort and breathe into them.
As you practice more try to match the rhythm of your breath to your walking rhythm.
Develop further by walking backwards.
Practice with a friend, take turns guiding each other, to develop trust and patience.

Record your observations below.

Know your heat

Triple warmer meridian energy encourages us to create internal harmony by finding, and walking, our own balanced path.

When triple warmer meridian energy lacks balance we can be 'all or nothing'.
Reflect on any times you have felt this way.
Do you dig your heels in, just to win?

Do some things make you hot in a 'positive' way, and others in a 'negative' way? What's the difference? Which do you prefer?

What does stubbornness achieve? Could this be achieved another way?

Pause for menopause

Taking a holistic view means playing the life-long game.
Exploring what can be done today to improve health and well being tomorrow.
For women life changes in 7 year cycles, for men it's 8 year cycles.
Consider the developments between these ages 0, 7, 14, 21, 28, 35, 42, 49, 56 and 63.
These changes are managed by hormones, which can be affected by various factors, including stress, nutrition, hydration, exercise and sleep.
Taking control of these aspects helps keep this sophisticated chemical system in balance, easing transitions through each stage.
Whilst hormonal changes are inevitable, menopausal symptoms are not.

After 40 menopause becomes the 'go-to' reason for every symptom experienced.

Match the symptoms below to their possible cause.
Tick all the causes that could apply for each symptom.

Symptom	Menopause	Common Cold	Low Blood Sugar	Stress
Mood swings				
Irritability				
Aggressive outbursts				
Crying spells				
Anxiety				
Tension				
Excessive sweating				
Depression				
Tiredness				
Forgetfulness				
Lack of concentration				
Difficulty coping				
Change in libido				
Loss of confidence				
Vulnerability				

It may be a surprise to learn that most of these symptoms can be attributed to each of the factors mentioned.
Taking better care of general health can improve symptoms that are perceived to be menopausal.
What menopausal symptoms are you expecting to experience/experiencing?
What else could be the cause?

_____
_____
_____

Tame your fire - Restore your cool

Hot flushes are viewed as the most common 'symptom' of menopause.
Commonly experienced as intense heat radiating across face, neck and chest.
Changes in hormone levels can confuse triple warmer meridian energy.
Hot flushes can be one response to this imbalance.
Try these simple hacks to tame your fire and restore your cool.

Reset the confusion and restore calm.
Do this every morning and evening and whenever a hot flush hits feel the heat subside.
With regular practice this can reduce in intensity and occurrence of hot flushes.

With the flat of your hand trace the following pathway 3 times on each side of the body.

Begin at the outer corner of the eye, move back to the top of the ear, smooth behind the ear, down the side of the neck, across the back of the shoulder blade, down the outside of the arm and off the ring finger.

Try this when a hot flush strikes.
Breathe away the heat with shatali pranayama breathing.
Caution: This exercise reduces blood pressure
Open mouth, roll tongue long ways and inhale.
Close mouth, flatten tongue and exhale through nose.
Repeat 5 -10 times

If your tongue won't roll, flatten it against the bottom of the mouth and breathe in through your teeth, close mouth and breathe out through your nose.

Certain foods create heat in the body whilst others are naturally cooling.
Try reducing heat creating foods in your diet and increasing naturally cooling foods.

Warming foods		Cooling foods	
Chilli pepper	Caffeine	Citrus fruits	Water
Refined Sugar	Cinnamon	Mint	Chrysanthemum
Ginger (dried)	Alcohol	Kelp	Watermelon
Black pepper	Garlic	Cucumber	Fermented Soya
Mustard Seed	Potatoes	Basil	Watercress
Cayenne Pepper	Carrots	Rooibos	Spinach

Reap the harvest of all your efforts with earth element

Earth is nourished by fire and feeds metal.

The ashes from the fire add nutrients to the earth.

The weight of the earth compresses down forming metals.

Earth is controlled by wood and controls water.

The roots of the wood hold the earth together.

Earth forms trenches, banks and boundaries to contain water.

Too much earth can drain productive activity with the need for continual reward, preventing sustained effort and restricting the flow of new ideas.

Too little earth can lead to activity without achievement and an inability to let go and move on.

Earth season is harvest (late summer), a time of golden sunsets, bringing in the harvest and a warm glow.

A season of fulfilment and reward.

Keep active and reflect on the fruits of your actions.

The meridians in the Earth element are Spleen (Yin) and Stomach (Yang).

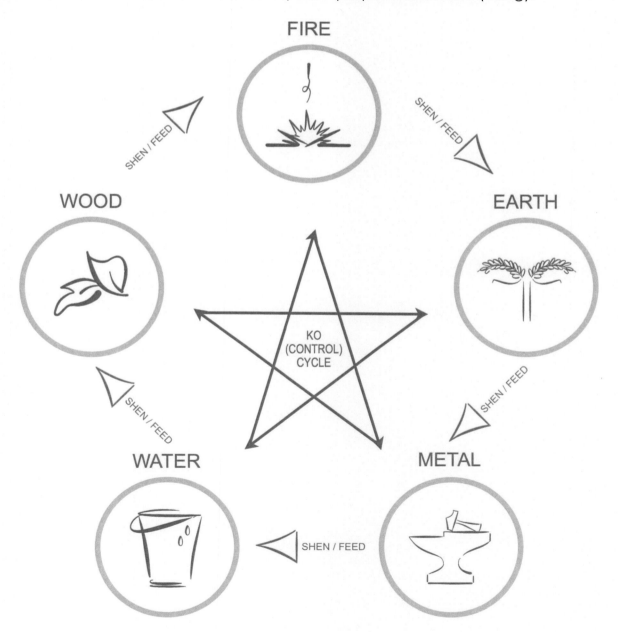

Use this page to record your thoughts and feelings. The words at the foot of the page describe emotions associated with the earth element.

Disgust **Rejection** Doubt Contentment Assured **Critic**
Consideration Approval **Indifference** *Cynical* **Deprivation**
Satisfaction Inclusive *Envy* Nausea *Sympathy*
Empathy Harmony **Hunger** *Faith* Confidence

Spleen Meridian Insights

Spleen is the yin meridian of the earth element.
It is also referred to as 'minister of the granary.

Spleen meridian energy is at it's height between 9am and 11am, but you can use these tips at any time of day to help you feel more secure and grounded.

Spleen meridian energy commands extraction and mobilisation of meridian energy from the stomach meridian to the lung meridian; where it blends with oxygen to create Qi (life force).

Spleen meridian is the palace of thoughts and intentions.
"If you can dream it you can do it" energy is hard at work here, bringing thoughts and intentions into form, so be careful what you wish for and consider the thoughts you create; focus on neutral and positive thinking.

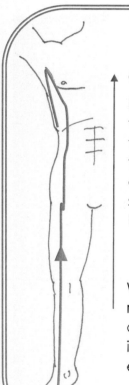

On both sides of the body

begin at the outside of the big toe, continue up the front of the shin, across the front of the thigh, up the body to the arm crease then down the side of the body to the bottom of the rib cage.

With a flat hand trace the meridian pathway 3 times to quieten the internal narrative, improve memory and enhance grounding feelings.

Take time to stop and smell the flowers.
Scent is evocative of memories and fragrance supports work with the spleen meridian.
Spleen meridian energy directs memories to kidney meridian for temporary storage then to heart meridian for long term storage.
Work with spleen meridian energy to help improve analytical thinking, cognition, intelligence, ideas generation, memory storage and recall.

Thoughts and ideas power the machinery that drives us.
For access to your idea pool support spleen meridian and get motoring.

Dealing with toxic thoughts, behaviours and emotions

When something is toxic it is destructive and harmful.

Toxic thoughts, behaviours and emotions can prevent us moving past trauma.

We continue to infect ourselves with ideas that pull sub-conscious triggers, setting off negative, internal programs.

We might tell ourselves we're 'stupid' for feeling scared or 'bad' for being late.

These judgements create self fulfilling prophecies.

Re-framing the way we speak to ourselves makes it easier to find a new perspective and let the toxic stuff go.

Listen to the words you use to speak to or about yourself.
Note them down in the left hand column, in the table below.
Reflect on the questions at the top of the other columns.

Word used	Is it kind?	How do you feel about it?	What could you say instead?

After you've chosen your new vocabulary (the words in the column on the right), try using these words for a few days.   Record your observations in the spaces below.

The truth about confidence

Confidence is closely associated with spleen meridian energy.
Poor confidence combines various emotional states, perceptions and behaviours into one 'super state', making confidence a game changer.

The key to self-confidence is developing faith and trust in ourselves.
Complete the following statements with as many positive statements as you can.

I believe I can _____
I believe I can _____
I believe I can _____
I believe I can _____
I believe I can _____
I believe I can _____
I believe I can _____
I believe I can _____
I believe I can _____
I believe I can _____
I believe I can _____
I believe I can _____
I believe I can _____
I believe I can _____

I trust myself to _____
I trust myself to _____
I trust myself to _____
I trust myself to _____
I trust myself to _____
I trust myself to _____
I trust myself to _____
I trust myself to _____
I trust myself to _____
I trust myself to _____
I trust myself to _____
I trust myself to _____
I trust myself to _____
I trust myself to _____

Every time we tell ourselves we lack confidence we reject our own skills and talents, undermining our trust and self belief.
Return to this page any time that happens, remind your self who you really are.

What if it all went right?

The future is an unwritten story, full of possibility and potential, we have the opportunity to write it as we wish.

We get caught up in 'negative imagining', creating a story full of monsters and pitfalls, killing any opportunities before they even start.

Give yourself permission to write as if everything goes right, follow the prompts round, how could the story go?

Start with an idea → What if it is well received? → ◯ → What will you do next? → ⬡ → What if that goes well? → ◯ → What if that succeeds? → ▢ → Where else could you go? → And then? → ⌇ → Where could this go? ✦

And then? ← ◯ ← And then? ← ⌇

Make a note here of the emotions you experience as you develop your 'happy ever after' story.
How does it feel to work in this way?
How do those emotions affect you?

_____
_____
_____
_____
_____
_____
_____
_____
_____
_____

Wake up your immune system

In late summer routine resumes for many.
The joy and freedom of the long summer vacation are over.
Feet that have been bare are squeezed into shoes.
Work and school uniforms are pressed, the burden of weighty bags are carried, daily timetables rule the day.
People are crammed back together in schools, on public transport and in offices.
Windows are closed (if they were ever opened) and coughs and colds proliferate.
Earth season is the time of the immune system.
Any neglect, through the year, can become more evident now.

This daily tip takes less than five minutes and stimulates your immune system to perk up and pay attention, ready to ward off unwelcome intruders.

 With a soft fist thump the space in the centre of your chest, on your sternum, for 20 seconds.

 Next, make like Tarzan and thump the space at the front of both shoulders, with soft fists, for 20 seconds.

 Finally, make like a monkey. With soft fists thump the side seams of your torso, in line with the underside of the breast, for 20 seconds.

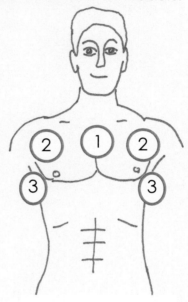

Other tips for warding off coughs, colds and other nasties.

Increase vitamin C intake.
Drink hot water with fresh lemon and grated ginger.
Try some turmeric- add to food or hot milk.
Reduce caffeine and alcohol intake.
Cut out refined sugar, go for natural sweetness instead.
Switch to a natural deodorant rather than an antiperspirant, perspiration is one of the bodies natural detox processes.
Keep moving.
As the nights draw in it's tempting to stay indoors, get outside for a walk during the day, enjoy the final rays of summer sunshine.

Celebrate to accumulate

Spleen meridian energy resonates with the satisfaction of harvest, the golden glow of accomplishment.

Acknowledging our accomplishments and the part we played in the outcome, is crucial to support, nurture and balance this meridian, creating feelings of inclusion, reassurance, confidence and fulfilment.

It life lacks sweetness, or your body craves it, try congratulating yourself for a job well done. Be sincere and acknowledge the part you played in the outcome.

Celebrate milestones as you go.
Break your task down into achievable steps.
Celebrate each accomplishment along the way.
Each celebration is life affirming, creating further impetus to keep going.
Use these spaces to record any accomplishments that have gone unrecognised.
Continue completing them as you achieve more steps along your journey.

Nourishment for spleen meridian energy

In Traditional Chinese Medicine the spleen is the 'minister of the granaries'; where grains are kept to dry, stored for use when nourishment is scarce.

Spleen meridian energy works similarly, keeping damp and infection away from that which nourishes us.

Spleen meridian energy is believed to be responsible for memory, cognition and intelligence. Try to focus on the memories that nourish you.

Work with spleen meridian energy to help improve your memory and recall.

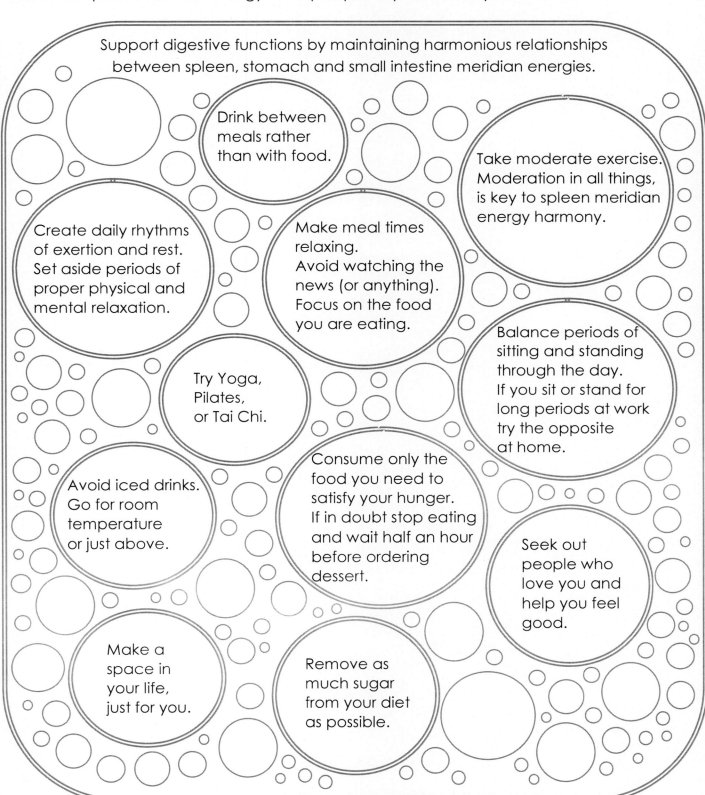

Support digestive functions by maintaining harmonious relationships between spleen, stomach and small intestine meridian energies.

- Drink between meals rather than with food.
- Take moderate exercise. Moderation in all things, is key to spleen meridian energy harmony.
- Create daily rhythms of exertion and rest. Set aside periods of proper physical and mental relaxation.
- Make meal times relaxing. Avoid watching the news (or anything). Focus on the food you are eating.
- Balance periods of sitting and standing through the day. If you sit or stand for long periods at work try the opposite at home.
- Try Yoga, Pilates, or Tai Chi.
- Avoid iced drinks. Go for room temperature or just above.
- Consume only the food you need to satisfy your hunger. If in doubt stop eating and wait half an hour before ordering dessert.
- Seek out people who love you and help you feel good.
- Make a space in your life, just for you.
- Remove as much sugar from your diet as possible.

Connect with the earth

Getting in touch with the earth is a great way to recharge spleen meridian energy and raise your mood.
The Traditional Chinese Medicine term for 'bad mood' translates to 'bad spleen energy'.
Working with spleen meridian energy eases the transition from summer to autumn.

Get outside in the late summer sunshine.
Tidy plants before autumn rolls round.
Collect and store any remaining herbs, fruits and vegetables.
Trim back any plants you want to do more next year.
Cut back creepers and ground cover plants, help them grow more vigorously next year.

Hug a tree.
Trees are powerhouses of energy.
In late summer they begin pulling sap in, from their leaves, recharging their internal reserves, ready to let go in autumn.
Place your palms against the trunk of a tree and breathe, experience the feeling this promotes.

Get active outside.
As the days cool it's the perfect time to go for a jog, a brisk walk, a game of golf, or just explore, outside.
Allow yourself to go somewhere new and take time to stop and breathe in the rich palette of late summer colours.

Walk, dance or stand, barefoot, on the earth.
Stand in mountain pose or on one leg at a time.
Feel your centre ground and focus.

Take a blanket and lie on the ground.
Lie on your front, support your head on your hands, focus on your breath.
Allow the earth beneath to support you as you centre and ground.
Experience a renewed sense of control.

Stomach meridian insights

Stomach meridian is the yang meridian of the earth element.
Also referred to as 'minister of the mill' and 'sea of nourishment'.

With a flat hand trace the meridian pathway 3 times on each side, whenever you want to calm emotional upset and enhance feelings of satisfaction and contentment.

On both sides of the body.
Begin just beneath the eye,
down to the chin,
up the cheek,
to the top edge of the forehead,
down the front of the face,
down the front of the neck,
out across the collar bone,
down the chest and abdomen,
across the front of the hip, down the front of the leg
to the end of the second toe.

The process of digestion begins in the mouth where food is chewed, mixing it with saliva, creating a slurry like substance called chyme.
Swallowing pushes the chyme down the oesophagus into the stomach where it mixes with acids that start to dissolve the food, particularly proteins.
The chyme is then pushed into the small intestine for further breakdown and absorption.
Peristalsis is like a Mexican wave, pushing food through the digestive process.
Peristalsis starts in the oesophagus when food is swallowed.

Stomach meridian energy reaches its zenith between 7 am and 9 am, eating a decent, nutritious breakfast nourishes both physically and emotionally.
Use these tips at any time of day to enhance feelings of personal fulfilment and self-confidence.
Stomach meridian energy works closely with the senses of taste, smell, sight and sound.
Taking time and space to engage fully with meals provides nourishment on a deeper level, improving sensations of satisfaction and reduces comfort eating.

Try eating food with your eyes closed and holding your nose.
Can you taste a difference?

The human stomach is a muscular, elastic, pear shaped 'bag' sitting in a 'J' shape.
It is approximately 30cms long and up to 15cms deep.

Nourish and glow

Personal nourishment is about more than the food we eat.
Our spiritual and emotional selves also require good quality input, to thrive and grow.

Consider your emotional and spiritual diet.
What do you incorporate into your life?
Tick any that you already do or intend to explore.

Activities	Do	Intend
Uplifting music.		
Aspirational reading.		
Strengthening exercise such as Yoga, Pilates, Tai Chi.		
Meditation or breath work.		
Things that make you smile.		
Rewards for a job well done.		
Quality time with friends/family.		
Authentic self-expression.		
Using emotional support.		
Relaxing therapies i.e. Massage, reflexology, reiki.		
Growth therapies i.e. kinesiology, counselling, CBT.		
Rhythmic exercise i.e. dance, Zumba.		
Play.		
Creative expression i.e. crafting, cooking, writing.		
Self exploration.		
Spiritual connection.		
Singing.		
Playing a musical instrument.		
Exercise for fun.		
Poetry.		
Journaling.		
Learning.		
Colour.		

What nourishment do these activities provide? Do you need something else to thrive?

_____
_____

Heal your inner child

Children have limited autonomy, gradually learning independence .
During unsettling, confusing or traumatic life events, lasting vulnerabilities can develop.
In adulthood, unconscious triggers wake latent responses, opening old wounds.
The expectation of adults to 'cope' compounds feelings of isolation.

The child we were lives within perpetually.
Whilst life experiences affect perspective, the individual remains, often masked by coping mechanisms, created in response to life lessons.
Embracing and healing the inner child can be an emotional and cathartic process.

Children are taught to be 'good' by encouraging and rewarding 'acceptable' behaviour.
Whilst 'unacceptable' behaviour is discouraged and, possibly, punished, creating an internal narrative, informing subsequent judgements, experiences and choices.
Exploring the definition of 'good' and 'bad' we are taught, in childhood, enables us to use wider criteria to inform our decision making as adults.

Explore your beliefs by completing the following statements.

Gardens are _____
Sport is _____
It is fun to _____
It is important that I _____
Women _____
Play is _____
Money means _____
Men _____
By age 40 a person _____

As a child what were you encouraged to do, achieve or pursue?

As a child what were you discouraged from doing or aspiring to?

How does this affect the choices you make as an adult?

Embracing the child within

The child within seeks validation, acceptance and succour.
Being hard or unkind to ourselves distresses the vulnerable child within.
With nowhere to access support, isolation increases and anxieties are magnified.
Some lessons we learned as children can be restrictive or destructive.
Exploring the internal narrative creates an opportunity to construct a new, more relevant narrative, supporting and encouraging growth, resilience and autonomy.

Which of these words do you use about yourself? Fill in any others in the blank bubbles.

Must, Push, Can't, Stupid, Force, Never, Don't, Hate, No, Fail, Should

Try altering your vocabulary for a week. Focus on including kind and supportive words.

Often, Interesting, Curious, Love, Might, Could, Enjoy, Sometimes, Try, Valid, Creative, Choose

Make some time and space to embrace and connect with the child within.
Give thanks and praise, forgive any naivety and lack of autonomy.
Update your inner child about your achievements and strengths.
Offer reassurance that, together, you made it through.
Communicate forgiveness for the past and hope for the future.
Use the space below to record your reflections.

Simple hacks to support stomach meridian energy

In Traditional Chinese Medicine the stomach meridian is the home of emotion, hence getting butterflies in your stomach when you're anxious and finding it difficult to eat anything, at times of stress.

Stomach meridian is referred to as 'the minister of the mill'.

If you're 'going through the mill', engage with stomach meridian energy to find resolution.

Support stomach meridian energy by having regular, uninterrupted, meals.
Avoid eating 'on the hop', sit down to eat whenever possible.

Assist your digestion by chewing foods well.

The stomach is an acid bath with no teeth.

Chewing mixes saliva with food, which begins to break it down.

Swallowing powers peristalsis, the 'wave' that helps food travel through the intestines.

The process of chewing, physically and metaphorically, involves getting 'a feel' for a situation and getting the taste of it.

Does a situation feel, smell or taste 'off'?

Allow yourself time to get the scent and 'chew it over' before deciding to swallow it down.

Consider situations for a short time then walk away.
Return later to explore some more.
Taking in too much emotional stimulation or information in one sitting feels overwhelming and can be hard to digest.

Reduce the size of meals through the day.

Breakfast like a king.   Lunch like a prince.   Dinner like a pauper.

Improve the health, function and hydration of the mouth, oesophagus and stomach by regularly drinking clear, pure water.

Great if foods, thoughts or emotions repeat on you.

These vital parts of the digestive process cannot separate water from hot drinks or sodas, that's the job of the small intestine.

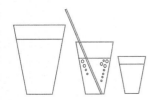

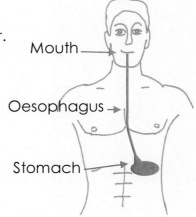

Mouth

Oesophagus

Stomach

Fulfilment and satisfaction

Stomach meridian energy encourages us to take satisfaction from our achievements.
Savouring the juicy fruits of our labours creates sweetness and gratification.
Celebrating our success is vital to increase motivation and stimulate gratitude.
An unmet need for gratification and acknowledgement can create insatiable demand.
This can manifest as chronic over consumption.
Acknowledge your accomplishments, respect your efforts, honour your self.
Comparisons discourage growth. Offer compassion, aspire to improve.

Try This: Write 10 statements to respect, acknowledge and honour different aspects of yourself.
Begin each statement "I honour my". The first one is started for you.

I honour my _____

_____
_____
_____
_____
_____
_____
_____
_____
_____

Reflect on any thoughts and emotions experienced in undertaking this exercise.
What did you encounter before, during and afterwards?
Did your experience alter?
What happens when you read back over the statements recorded above?

Look around

The average adult human head weights approximately 5kg.
Many of the muscles that support the head are in the neck and shoulder area, which tenses under stress; causing headaches and upper back discomfort.
Stomach meridian energy helps us to hold our head up high.
Try these simple exercises to support stomach meridian energy, promote calm and focus, while releasing tension from the head, neck and shoulders.

If possible, sit in a comfortable, supported position.
Place both feet flat on the floor or stand with your feet hip distance apart.
Take a moment to check in with your body.
Take note of any areas of physical or emotional tension, pain or stress.
Breathing naturally only move as far as is comfortable.
Repeat the suggestions below, on both sides, 3 times

Look straight ahead.
Turn your head slowly to look over your left shoulder.
Slowly return to face the front.

Look straight head.
Turn your head to slowly look over your right shoulder.
Slowly return to the centre.

Look straight ahead.
Slowly drop the weight of your head towards the chest.
Breathe allowing your head to relax forward and down.
Slowly lift your head to look forward.
Gently drop the weight of your head backwards.
Breathe allowing the head to relax back and down.
Slowly return to centre.
Repeat 3 times.

Now observe any previous areas of stress. Record your thoughts and observations here.

_____
_____
_____
_____

Monitor your hidden intake

It's easy to reflect on the physical nourishment taken in.
Each day we also take on other 'stuff', like thoughts, opinions, ideas and emotions.
These might lift us up, have no effect or drag us down.

Key
- ↑ Lifted mood
- ↔ No effect
- ↓ Depressed mood

Choose a day to reflect on the effect of everything you take on board.
Record each item in the relevant area.
Put an arrow next to it to record the effect.

Media (social, TV, radio, print)

Loved ones (people, pets, passions)

Work (paid, voluntary)

Social (sports, friends, activities)

Reflect on your observations below.
How does your intake nourish you?
Do you need to adjust your emotional diet to improve your personal nourishment?

Let go and breathe easy with metal element energy

Metal is nourished by earth and feeds water.

The weight of the earth compresses down forming metals.

Water filters through this compressed layer, filtering out impurities and making it safe to drink once more.

Metal is controlled by fire and controls wood.

The heat of fire smelts the metal ore, making it workable.

Sharpened metal blades cut down wood, keeping it manageable.

Too much metal can create over sensitivity and responsibility for situations beyond our control, impairing realisation of the self, preventing engagement with change.

Too little metal can rob us of personal satisfaction and fulfilment, leading to an over inflated sense of self and disproportionate fear in the face of perceived danger.

Metal season is autumn, a time letting go of that which is no longer needed, allowing it to fall away and rot, enabling residual nutrients to be absorbed.

A season of reflection.

Remember your achievements, get ready for the new dream.

The meridians in the metal element are Lung (Yin) and Large intestine (Yang).

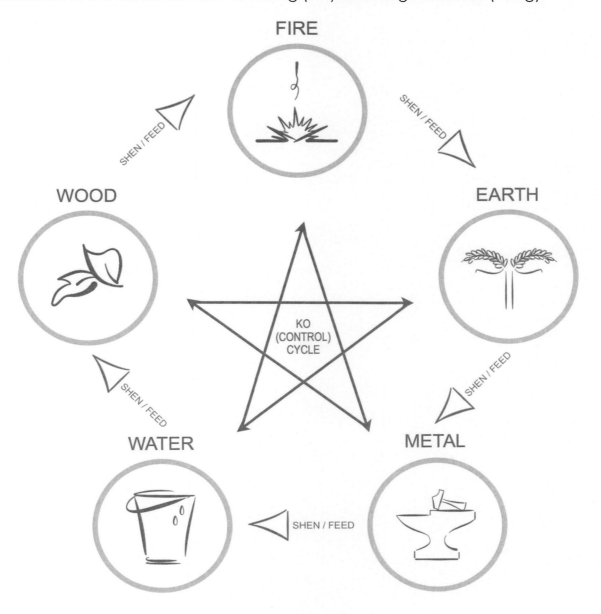

Use this page to record your thoughts and feelings. The words at the foot of the page describe emotions associated with the metal element.

Depressed Regret Modesty **Release** **Connection** Dignity **Indifferent** Humility Interested *Compassion* **Merciful** Insular Sad Cheerful *Guilt* Openness *Distraction* **Tolerance** **Freedom** *Haughty* Enthusiastic

Lung meridian insights

Lung meridian is the yin meridian of the metal element.
It is also known as 'the prime minister', 'the priest' or 'the minister of heaven'.

Lung meridian energy is responsible for establishing the foundation of Qi for the entire body.
Lung meridian energy also contains diaphragm energy which is responsible for regulating energy flow throughout the entire system; regulating yin and yang flows, whilst embodying them simultaneously.
Diaphragm energy allows spontaneous access to a powerful yang aspect of the yin lung meridian energy, enabling the ability to sprint, when necessary.

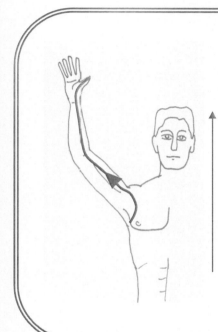

On both sides of the body start at the space below the front of the shoulder and above the rib cage, follow up the inside of the front of the arm to the end of the thumb.

With a flat hand trace the meridian pathway 3 times on each side, to balance feelings of openness and cheer.
Energise and mobilise the meridian by stretching both arms out wide, high and back.

Lung meridian energy peaks between 3 am and 5 am.
Use the tips on these pages at any time of day to help you breathe easy, sleep well and connect with your inspiration.

The average person takes over 23,000 breaths every day.
Take 5 minutes out each day to focus on your breath to find peace and calm.

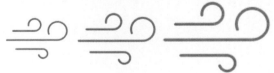

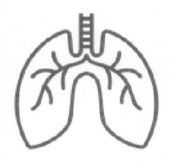

The construction of the tubular network inside the lungs is mirrored in the trunk and branches of deciduous trees.
This symbiotic relationship with trees for pure oxygen creation and carbon dioxide disposal is essential for human survival.

Releasing weighty emotional armour

Life is a series of learning opportunities.

Ideally we learn lessons, form supportive frameworks for growth, whilst releasing the weight of the experiences.

In reality we can carry the emotional armour of our encounters, long after battles are over.

This armour inhibits spontaneity and creativity, causing rigidity and stunting aspirations.

Embrace the life affirming power of lung meridian energy to create supportive frameworks and release the weight that holds you back.

Armour can sometimes be difficult to see.

Identify yours by reflecting on any negative beliefs containing words such as 'always', 'every', 'all' or 'never'.

Consider your vocabulary and record your 'armour' words/phrases below.

_____
_____
_____
_____
_____

Next, record one of your personal 'armour' beliefs in the space below.

I believe _____
_____

Now consider where that belief came from. It may result from several experiences. Record your observations below. Put dates to them if you can.

_____
_____
_____
_____
_____
_____
_____

What was the constructive lesson to learn from those experiences?
How does this differ from your personal armour belief?

_____
_____
_____
_____
_____
_____
_____

Try some of the exercises on the next page to release the weight of the emotional armour, whilst integrating the lesson into your personal toolkit.

Stretch and glow

Stretching is a great tonic for lung meridian energy.
Stretching supports breathing, calms the mind, tones muscles and restores harmony.
Try these gentle stretches and experience calm revitalisation.
Remember to listen to your body and work within your limits.

Stand with feet hip distance apart.
Keep back straight, knees soft and shoulders down and back.
Inhale.
Extend both arms straight above the head.
Exhale.
Keeping arms outstretched, over head, move hands 1m apart.
Inhale.
Keeping arms outstretched lower arms to shoulder level.
Exhale.
Keeping arms outstretched bring palms together, at chest height.
Repeat sequence 3 times.

Stand with feet hip distance apart.
Keep back straight, knees soft and shoulders down and back.
Hold both arms outstretched at the side of the body, at shoulder height, palms facing forward.
Inhale.
As you **exhale** swing the right hand across the front of the body to touch the left palm (or as close as you can get).
Inhale as you swing the right hand back to starting position.
As you **exhale** swing the left arm across the front of the body to touch the right palm (or as close as you can get).
Inhale as you swing the left hand back to starting position.
Repeat 5 times

Stand with feet hip distance apart.
Keep back straight and shoulders down and back.
Press palms together, in front of the body, at chest height.
Inhale and exhale, deeply and slowly.
Maintain pressure against palms, repeat 10 cycles of breath.

Complimentary jewels

Compliments are the sparkling jewels of human communication.
Precious gifts, offered without agenda.
Give them, take them, treasure them, allow compliments to brighten the day.

Try this:
Consider some of the people in your life, what do you admire about them?
Next time you see them, offer them a compliment.

Person	Compliment

Reflect on your experience of offering a compliment and their response.
Consider how this exercise affected you.

Compliments and praise are direct expressions of gratitude and admiration.
Graceful acceptance demonstrates respect of ourselves and others.
Practice accepting compliments and praise.

How do you respond when you receive compliments on the following?

Appearance

Clothing

Skills/Talents/Achievements

Try this: On receiving a compliment say 'thank you'.
Record your observations below.

Reading, writing and reality

Breathing has a natural pause between each action, distinctly separating inhalation and exhalation.

A choice to take on board inspiration, replacing and releasing that which no longer serves.

A pause where peace, cleansing and integrity converge, informing our world view.

It is easy to absorb what we read without conscious choice, especially when information, rhetoric and opinion are so easily shared.

Reading is like a breath in and writing, a breath out.

The trouble with having an open mind, of course, is that people will insist on coming along and trying to put things in it.

Terry Pratchett

What methods do you utilise to update your world view?

| Popular press ☐ | Social media ☐ | Industry journals ☐ | Text books ☐ |
| Essays ☐ | Technical websites ☐ | Generic websites ☐ | Research papers ☐ |

Using the space below consider any information, opinions or rhetoric that do not serve you. What could you free yourself from? Where did you acquire them?

_____
_____
_____
_____

Try different methods to cleanse and clear your space to keep it free of out dated ideas, opinions and rhetoric.

- Journaling
- Write a blog
- Jottings
- Write poetry
- Essays
- Letter writing

Consider musing on a theme; be broad, allow your mind to wander.
Express yourself and give yourself permission to find your authentic voice.
Here are some suggestions to get you started.

- Individuality
- Blue
- Silence
- Power
- Beauty
- Plants
- Water
- Art
- Love
- Sleep
- Space
- Joy

The healing power of breath

Few people are ever taught to breathe.

The autonomic process kicks in and is mostly ignored, until something goes wrong.

Working with the breath can be extremely cathartic.

With the average adult taking around 20,000 breaths each day, that's plenty of opportunities for healing.

Allow yourself 30 minutes for this exercise.

Find a space where you can sit comfortably without being disturbed.

First practice making a sighing noise as you breathe out.

Repeat a couple of times, notice any changes in the noise each time.

Next think of an idea, belief, criticism or opinion you'd like to release. (refer to the emotional armour exercise for ideas).

Take a deep breath.

Imagine the idea, belief, criticism or opinion being expelled from your mouth as you breathe out, with a big sigh.

Repeat several times for each idea, belief, criticism or opinion you wish to release.

Note any changes in the sighing as you progress. Record your observations below.

_____
_____
_____
_____
_____

Imagine a belief, opinion, idea, criticism or experience you wish to release.

Give it a shape, a colour, a size and find the place where it sits in your body.

Now visualise waves of water washing over it, dissolving it.

With each new wave take a deep breath, breathe out the water in which the trauma is dissolved.

Imagine the droplets rushing from your mouth as you exhale, see them float away on the air.

Continue until the shape you originally imagined has dissolved away.

Record your observations below.

_____
_____
_____
_____
_____
_____

Nourish lung meridian energy

Add pungent flavours to your diet as autumn takes hold, to stoke your inner fire and help prevent mucus formation.

Wake up the palette and stimulate the senses, add interest to a potentially bland, store cupboard diet.

Heat a mug of nut or oat milk in a pan, add 1 teaspoon of ground cinnamon and a good sprinkle of freshly grated nutmeg.
Add honey to taste.
Stir or whisk continually until hot.
Enjoy as a delicious, dairy and caffeine free, warming drink.

Cut down on cold dairy products, orange and tomato juices, to reduce mucus formation.

Add plenty of roughly torn fresh mint leaves to boiling water, leave to infuse for 5 minutes before drinking.

Add a tablespoon of horseradish to mashed potato to top an autumn cottage pie.

Simple pesto sauce for pasta
In a small blender combine
Handful of pine nuts
Hand full of torn fresh basil leaves
2 cloves of garlic
12 black olives roughly chopped
Zest and juice of 1/2 a lemon
Glug of olive oil
2 Tablespoons of pasta water
Blitz together, combine with pasta,
Enjoy.

In a mug combine
Grated 1" cube of fresh ginger
Juice and zest of 1/2 a lemon
Fill with boiling water.

Simple watercress soup
Sautee 1 large, finely chopped onion, in a little oil, until translucent.
Sieve in 1 teaspoon flour and mix to a roux.
Gradually incorporate 400ml water, milk or milk alternative, stir continually until thickened.
Add 3 bunches of fresh watercress (approx. 400g) washed and roughly chopped.
Simmer for a couple of minutes.
Remove from the heat, liquidise and serve.

Add 2 cloves of freshly chopped garlic to your savoury recipes.

Start the day with porridge (made with water), drizzle with a little honey, top with a handful of seeds.
Sprinkle ground cinnamon and freshly grated nutmeg for extra flavour and warmth.

Releasing regret

Regret is a mixture of sadness and disappointment, about an act or omission, something that didn't go to plan.

Whilst it is important to acknowledge and learn from the experience, carrying regret only reinforces feelings of inadequacy, damaging confidence and self-esteem, creating substantial barriers to progress.

All that is possible, in any of these situations, is to take responsibility, apologise/make amends, where possible, and move on.

Moving on requires willingness, compassion, forgiveness and mercy.

> Imagine you are on the receiving end of the act or omission that you regret.
> Consider how you would respond when the other person expresses their regret.
> Reflect on how you might feel, what you would do, the words you would use.
> _____
> _____
> _____
> _____

We are often more judgemental and less forgiving of ourselves, than we are with others. Harsh internal judgements feed the inner critic, eroding our sense of self from the inside. Try the exercise below to be kinder to yourself and release regret.

> Fill out the information in the letter below, it is a letter to yourself.
> Once completed, read it aloud, to yourself.
> Record your observations in the space below the letter.

Dear (insert your name),

I love you.

I am sorry I (insert act or omission),

I understand I (consequence of act or omission)

I take responsibility for that.

I appreciate that I cannot change what is passed, in future I will (change of action or omission).

To make amends I will (insert suitable offer of help).

(Sign your name)

Large intestine meridian insights

Large intestine meridian is the yang meridian of the metal element.
It is also referred to as 'minister of transportation'.

Large intestine meridian energy is at it's peak between 5 am and 7 am, time to get up and get on with the new day.
Use these tips at any time of day to help release the clutter from the past and embrace whatever today has to offer.

Large intestine meridian energy is concerned with getting rid of the old rubbish that has been hanging around for too long, it's time to empty the garbage.

Old ideas, thoughts and beliefs can get stuck in the large intestine causing low mood, lethargy and low self esteem.
Treat yourself to a good clear out by regularly using the tips in this section.

With a flat hand trace the large intestine meridian pathway 3 times on each side of the body, to assist the release of that which no longer has value.

On both sides of the body begin on the
thumb side of the index finger,
continue down the hand to the wrist,
outside the back of the arm,
across the shoulder,
up the side of the neck,
across the cheek.
Finish at the side of the nose.

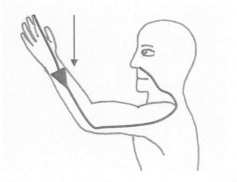

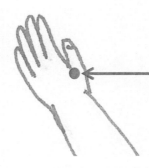

The acupressure point, large intestine 4, is located on the fleshy web between thumb and forefinger, on both hands.
Press and firmly hold this point to alleviate headaches, disperse wind and relieve pain.
NB: This point is not suitable for use during pregnancy.

Clean from the inside out

Large intestine is a tube of dense muscle, squeezing the last of the water out of our food and updating the brain about any incoming bacteria, viruses or other threats.

Large intestine houses a vast colony of useful bacteria and gut flora, it's a busy, happening centre of activity and information.

Try this large intestine work out to stimulate waste elimination; especially anything that's outstayed it's welcome, including emotional waste, physical and biochemical gunk. Always aim to do this exercise on an empty stomach and never straight after a meal.

 Top Tip
Large intestine meridian energy is most active between 5am and 7am. Incorporate this into your daily, morning routine for maximum benefit.

Grab a standard tennis ball or similar.

Starting on the front of your right hip, follow the pathway in the diagram, place your tennis ball on the start point and work along the journey of the large intestine, gently, but firmly, make small circles with the ball.

Use the flat of your hand to move the ball round and along. Always massage in the direction of the arrows, towards the anus.

If an area feels congested, focus on it for a moment before moving on.

It is more beneficial to work slowly to release waste and encourage it to move on, than to focus for too long on one spot.

Finish on the left hip, lift the ball away, replace on the right hip and repeat the process 3 - 5 times.

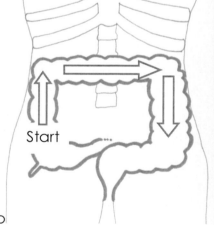

Regular practice improves large intestine muscle tone and promotes waste elimination.

Think of the large intestine as a one-way street, focus on moving everything towards the exit.

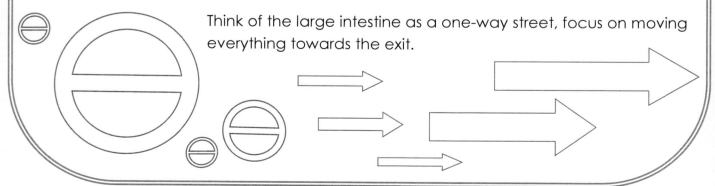

De-clutter your life

De-cluttering creates wiggle room.
Make space in your life to shake your funky stuff.
Preserve what is precious and dump what is not.
What emotions come up for you when you consider de-cluttering?
Record them in the spaces below.

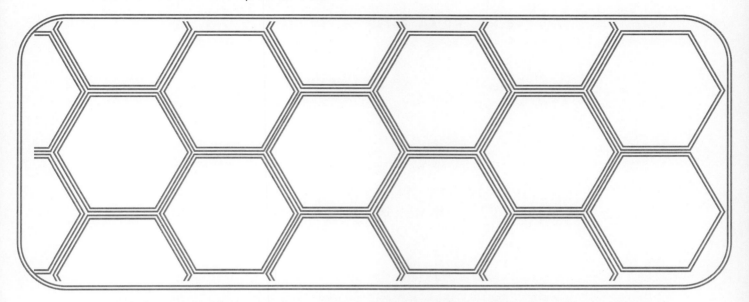

Try these simple tips to help avoid overwhelm and make space.

Poddling means 'to move or travel in a leisurely manner; amble', it is the perfect antidote to 'death by lists'.
Combine your poddle with the 'one touch rule' and focus on what you find, rather than creating unrealistic demands.

The 'one touch rule' states 'when you pick an item up, deal with it'.
If it's for sale, list it. If it's rubbish, bin it. If it's for the charity shop, donate it.
Make full use of kerbside collection charity bags, aim to put one out every day/week.
Set yourself a daily target.
Deal with 10 things each day.
Improve focus, reduce stress and clutter.
The impact is quickly apparent and very motivating.

Give everything an expiration date.
Have you worn it, read it, eaten it or used it in the last 12 months?
Unsure how long you've had something for?
Write today's date on it and move on to something else - this practice is very revealing and saves time trying to remember how long ago you acquired or used an item.

If you need support ask for it.
Remember to congratulate yourself for everything you deal with.

Would-a, should-a, could-a

Should : Verb 'used to indicate obligation, duty, or correctness, typically when criticising someone's actions'.

'Should' is an emotive and destructive word, containing undertones of failure and awakening the wounded child, alive within us.
Using 'should' triggers deep held feelings of rejection, inadequacy and lack of autonomy, breathing life back into those memories, awakening them in the present.

Simple changes can significantly improve self-esteem, confidence and relationships.
By replacing one word with another we create space, enhance motivation, improve momentum and build success.

Try this to break the emotional cycle and build self-esteem.
Start by completing the sentences in the top table, an example has been completed for you.

I tell myself I should….	when I don't, I feel….	and when I feel like that I….
Go to the gym, get fit	*guilty and lazy*	*eat chocolate.*

For each sentence in the table above create a 'could' sentence.
Record your observations on how this feels.

Given the choice I could...	this feels...	and when I feel like that I...
park further away, walk	*empowering*	*am invincible.*

Reflect on this exercise below, consider how using 'should' affects you and what difference 'could' and 'would' language might make.

Chase away the blues

Large intestine corresponds to the autumn season in the northern hemisphere. The reduction of light and temperature can impact mood, leading to feeling 'blue' for some, and more extreme depression in others.

Working on the elements, as they change through the course of the year, can support the transitions, through the seasons.

Try these tips and techniques to help improve mood.

Facial expressions directly affect mood, fake it till you make it and smile.

If smiling is too hard, place a pen horizontally between your back teeth, this activates the same muscles stimulating endorphin release.

Take a full body stretch and feel the difference.
Stretching releases feel good endorphins, promoting relaxation.

Go outside

Breathe

Ditch the duck face

Walk

Sunlight improves immunity, sleep, mood, reaction times and brain function.
It regulates hormones and behaviour.
It's a source of Vitamin D and stimulates melatonin production, also known as the 'sleep' hormone.

Drink a cup of peppermint tea

Remove sunglasses

Move

Spend 30 minutes in daylight

Laugh

Try Mustard Bach Flower Essence, a mood improver.

Surviving depression

Depression comes in many forms, for various reasons.
Engage with medical professionals to create a supportive treatment process.
The ideas in this book give you additional tools you can use to support yourself.

Emotional resilience is the pay off for a life of varied experiences, but it can come at a very high cost.
Deliberate self-care is crucial, especially during traumatic times.

Aim to spend at least 30 minutes outside, daily.
The positive effect of being outside can last up to 7 days .
Gardening, hanging up laundry, walking the dog, walking, listening to nature, are all great excuses for getting outside.
For maximum benefit allow your face to be in the light.

In Traditional Chinese Medicine (TCM) depression is believed to come from the suppression of anger, leading to the suppression of all other emotions.
The human psyche is unable to discriminate between expressing some emotions and not others.
Refer to the liver meridian energy chapter for tips on expressing and releasing anger.

Exploring the issues underlying your depression, with a trained counsellor can be very beneficial, if exhausting.
Be prepared to take time navigating your way through compassionately.
Witnessing what is happening is a powerful acknowledgement and start of the healing process.

Witnessing is compassionate observation, enabling us to create a way through the situation, rather than engaging in a tug-of-war.
As soon as we give up fighting against depression and start working with the messages our system is trying to communicate, the way out becomes clearer.
Focus on building bridges not barricades.

Loss and forgiveness

Grief, anger and regret are all natural emotional responses to loss.
Something or someone that occupied a significant space in our lives is no longer there.
It can take a year to begin to acknowledge the adjustments required.
Feelings of loss can be much more acute on special days.
Acknowledging the impact of loss, and offering forgiveness, is an important step.

It's normal to experience various emotions as a result of loss and to be less kind to ourselves as a consequence.
It's important to make space to acknowledge these and offer forgiveness.
Forgiveness to ourselves, the circumstances and all involved.
Use this space to identify any feelings and associations you experience.
An example has been completed to get you started.

When *my grandmother died*
I *regretted not being with her on her last day*
I forgive *myself, I was too far away to get there*

When
I
I forgive

When
I
I forgive

When
I
I forgive

When
I
I forgive

Record your observations and reflections, about this exercise, in the space below.

Feed your gut

The large intestine is a muscle, it needs hydration and exercise to work efficiently. Eating hydrating and bulking foods improves tone and function, easing elimination.

Porridge (made with water), water soaked chia seeds, cracked flax seeds and physillium husks all absorb water, transporting it through the digestive tract to the gut, where the rough edges chip faecal deposits away from the lining of the large intestine, clearing the gut wall of decaying matter.

Bitter flavours supress our appetite for sweet foods.

Bitter foods create a hostile environment for unwelcome bacteria, flora and parasites.

Bitter flavours stimulate the digestive process, including the secretion of bile to break down fats, the undulation of the oesophagus (peristalsis) and liver function.

Add bitter foods to your diet, like citrus fruits including yellow grapefruit and lemons, cauliflower, brussel sprouts, endive, broccoli, rocket and ginger.

What gut friendly foods will you include in your diet?

In the 1920s and 30s angostura bitters were popular in pre-dinner cocktails, referred to as 'digestifs'.

Dark chocolate and coffee

Red wine

Watercress

Aubergine

Green tea

Citrus fruits

Broccoli

Bramley apples

Peppers

Release fear and dream the dream of the future

Water is nourished by metal and feeds wood.

Water is cleansed and filtered as it permeates through the compressed metal layer, absorbing essential minerals.

Water feeds the roots of wood enabling growth.

Water is controlled by earth and controls fire.

Earth forms banks and trenches to contain water.

Water is used to douse the fire.

Too much water can lead to anxiety, fear for the future and excessive day dreaming, which does not translate to action.

Too little water can lead to poor self esteem, aversion to change and inability to move on from the past.

Water season is Winter, a time of short, short days and long, long nights where, before electricity, life would slow down, allowing time for reflection and rest. When we could sleep for long periods, taking in little and dreaming in the dream for the next cycle.

A season of resolving the past and making resolutions for the future.

Let go of the past and dream the dream of the future.

The meridians in the Water element are Kidney (Yin) and Bladder (Yang).

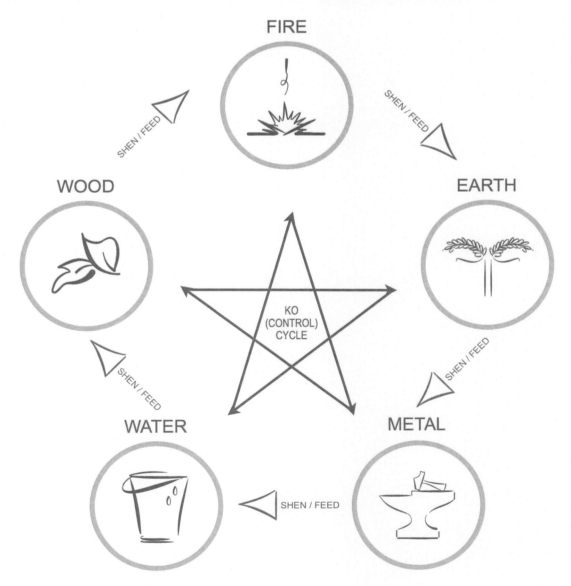

Use this page to record your thoughts and feelings. The words at the foot of the page describe emotions associated with the water element.

Cautious *loyal* *Deep* Flowing **Trust** **Fluid** Intuitive
Inspired *Resolute* Capable *Decisive* **Inadequate** Panic
Anxious Patience *Secure* **Creative** Restless
Stubborn Peace *Dream* Reckless **Brave**

Kidney Meridian Insights

Kidney meridian is the yin meridian of the water element.

Referred to as 'minister of power', 'reservoir of energy' & 'seat of courage and willpower'.

Kidney Meridian is a significant reservoir of essential energy (Qi) within the human body.

Imbalances can manifest as chronic fatigue and excess anxiety.

Use the tips in this section to help keep your personal reservoir full.

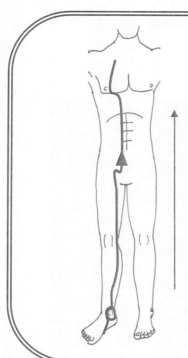

Kidney meridian pathway runs on both sides of the body.

Start on the ball of the foot, up the inside of the foot arch, sweep above, back and around the front of the ankle bone, up the inside of the calf and thigh,
across the outside edge of the pubic bone,
in across the front of the abdomen,
sweep up to the inside end of the collar bone (the knobbly bits on the front of the chest just below the neck).

With a flat hand trace the meridian pathway 3 times on each side, for support in times of anxiety.

Great when your internal powerhouse needs a boost.

Human beings have 2 kidneys, located at the back of the body, one on each side, at waist level.

Each kidney is between 10 and 12.5cms long, with approximately 1 million filtration units.

The kidneys process your blood plasma twice every hour, that's about 10 litres every hour.

Kidneys purify the blood by filtering out waste products and shunting them into the bladder, ready for excretion.

Kidney meridian energy is at it's height between 5pm and 7pm when we might need a 'second wind' or a 'Nana nap'.

Use the tips in this chapter at any time of day to improve energy levels, fill your internal energy store, increase calm and reduce anxiety.

Kidney meridian energy also includes the energy of the adrenal glands, which sit just above the kidneys.

Adrenal glands secrete a variety of essential hormones, including adrenaline, reducing stress has a significant impact on kidney meridian energy.

Embrace the frequency of water

Dr Masaru Emoto exposed water molecules to different words, frequencies and emotions, freezing the water and examining the crystals.

He found different input created different crystals, surmising that water holds a memory of the vibration it is exposed to.

Every word we speak carries a vibration that then ripples through us.

Since we are over 70% water, those vibrations can resonate within us at a cellular level.

So, by changing our personal vocabulary we can quickly change the way we feel.

Try this: Consider a time something didn't go to plan.
What negative words did you think/say to yourself? How did you feel?
How would you prefer to feel? What words/actions would create that feeling?
There's a completed example to help. Try some for yourself.

When things don't go to plan I tell myself *I am a fool, I must try harder.*
Then I feel *inadequate and lazy.*
I would prefer to feel *supported, able to learn from my efforts and experiences.*
I can achieve this by using words like: *What would I do differently next time?*

When things don't go to plan I tell myself _____
Then I feel _____
I would prefer to feel _____
I can achieve this by using words like: _____

When things don't go to plan I tell myself _____
Then I feel _____
I would prefer to feel _____
I can achieve this by using words like: _____

When things don't go to plan I tell myself _____
Then I feel _____
I would prefer to feel _____
I can achieve this by using words like: _____

Water, water, everywhere

Water is the most abundant constituent of the human body.
Human beings are 70% water and our blood is 92% water.
Every bodily process relies heavily on water, water is the lynchpin of all that we are.

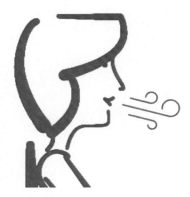

Every day we lose nearly 1litre of water, through breathing and perspiration.

Dehydration is stressful.
Drinking enough water, every day, reduces stress from the inside.
Water lubricates every bodily process, keeps our juicy bits moist, reducing blood pressure increasing the ability to think, focus, concentrate and perform.

Air conditioning , caffeine, stress, alcohol, smoking, exercise, sugar and heating use more water and can create dehydration.
Reduce your exposure or increase your water intake to maintain balance.

Try this: Take the daily 8 glass challenge.
Drink 8 x 250ml glasses of water each day for a week.

Record any changes for example concentration, emotional and physical health, sleep patterns, sleep quality, skin condition, stamina, mobility, weight, eating patterns.

Space 8 glasses through the day, this table might help.

Day	Observations
1	
2	
3	
4	
5	
6	
7	

Time	250ml
07:00	
08:00	
10:00	
12:00	
14:00	
16:00	
19:00	
21:00	

Cleaning your internal storage space

Kidney time is perfect for cleansing the space that was occupied by any restrictive or weighty thoughts, beliefs or emotions.

Think of your body as a bucket accumulating a layer of muck each day.
Cleansing the bucket of a lifetime of ingrained muck could be messy.
Quickly filling the bucket with water stirs up the muck, contaminating all the water.
The kidneys, liver and excretory organs work harder to detoxify and clean the water.
This creates physical symptoms, like headaches, making it harder to persevere.
The disturbed muck of all the behaviours, thoughts and beliefs settles back in the system.

A more effective method is to slowly pour a little extra water into the bucket, every day.
The extra water gradually loosens the debris, allowing the body to gently excrete toxins.
Over a period of time the system is transformed.
The water stays clear and a more gentle healing process is experienced.

Try this:
Focus on keeping personal internal storage clear by changing your responses to stress.

Stress is caused by a perceived inability to effect change.
If we cannot change a situation, we can choose to change how we engage with it.

Step 1: Identify a situation causing you stress: (Be specific) _____
_____
_____
_____

Step 2: Why does it stress you? _____
_____
_____
_____

Step 3: What action can you take to effect change? _____
_____
_____
_____

Step 4: How can you engage with it differently? _____
Avoid it? _____
Respond differently to it? _____
Question it? _____
Focus on something else? _____

The mystery of dreamtime

Use kidney energy to reflect.
Consider the water as a mill pond, so flat and pristine you can see your reflection.
When you look who do you see?
What stories are you making up that prevent your true reflection from shining out?
Is it time to reinvent yourself and allow a different aspect to take the spotlight?

Whatever you can do, or dream you can do, begin it.
Boldness has genius, power, and magic in it.

W. H. Murray

Sleep provides the time to process thoughts and experiences.
Hibernation is a space of suspended animation, when heart rate slows and input is nominal. This reduced activity creates an opportunity for our minds to reflect and explore, allowing ideas and concepts room to grow, without restriction, judgement or commitment.
Dreamtime is a fabulous space for bringing in the next idea or dream.
It is not necessary to make any decisions until spring, when nature gets busy planning, planting the seeds of the next adventure.

Try these simple ideas to get more from the deeper sleep of winter

As you close your eyes say aloud what you want to resolve whilst you sleep.
Use your dreamtime to create innovative solutions to problems, conflicts or relationships.
Ask 'who', 'what', 'where', 'when' or 'how' questions.
Gall-bladder energy is nourished by the water element, it loves juicy
questions and enjoys finding ideas while you rest.

Keep a pen and paper by the bed.
On waking record as much about your dreams as you remember.

Switch off the noise.
Water time is a time of quiet reflection.
Try driving, running, showering or cooking in silence.
Give space for any ideas trying to get through.

Doodle.
Invest in some coloured pens and plain paper, give yourself permission to wander while you doodle.
Fire up your creative brain, let new ideas flow.

Keep calm & carry on

Anxiety sets off an uncomfortable autonomic process.
Heart rate and breathing accelerate while concentration and physical control decrease.
Once the program is running there seems to be no way out.
However, there are exit points at every stage.
Try them and record your experiences.

Record your thoughts here

Real/imagined event. Body perceives threat.

EXIT POINT
Rewrite the story. What is actually happening?

Danger signals fly round the body.

EXIT POINT
Name 10 things you can see.

Brain engages PANIC mode.

EXIT POINT
Focus on the breath, exhale fully before each in breath.

Heart rate increases sending more blood to large muscles, ready to fight or flee.

EXIT POINT
Focus on the breath, inhale fully before each out breath.

Body pumps adrenaline to speed up breathing & heart rate. Perspiration increases. Bladder & bowel void. Appetite reduces.

EXIT POINT
Slowly sip a 250ml glass of cold water.

Who do you think you are?

Ego creates, maintains and reinforces personal identity.

In Traditional Chinese Medicine ego resides in the kidney meridian energy.

The struggle between conforming to the tribe and maintaining individuality can lead to isolation, self-doubt, indecision, insecurity and even phobias.

These emotions all indicate disharmony in kidney meridian energy.

Restore personal cohesion by working on the vitality of kidney meridian energy.

Try this exercise:

Record 12 positive, current statements about yourself

How does that feel?

I am
I am
I am
I am
I am
I am
I am
I am
I am
I am
I am
I am

Recognition of talents, skills, gifts and expertise changes our perspective.
It's time to transform the narrative.

Try this: How do you usually describe yourself?
Try using positive, constructive words. Who could you allow yourself to become?.

useless   *becomes*   *learning*
              becomes
              becomes
              becomes
              becomes
              becomes
              becomes

Breathing and other simple kidney meridian hacks

Kidneys are located in the low back, just above waist level.
Kidneys regulate body temperature.
Keep them warm by wearing a layer that covers them.
A simple hack to staying healthy.

Find a comfortable, seated position.
Place a squash ball, or similar, under the ball of one foot.
Press down with medium pressure, maintain this as you slowly
rotate the ball clockwise 10 times and then anti-clockwise 10 times.
Repeat on the other foot.

Use an alarm clock, even for a nap, allow the
body and mind to sleep and rest completely.

Walk barefoot on the ground
as often as possible.

Alternate nostril breathing gently calms the mental, emotional and physical body.
Great for reducing anxiety and overwhelm, finding solutions, improving concentration and promoting restful sleep.
Whenever you need to reset, regroup and refresh, this technique ticks all the boxes.

Find a comfortable position, seated or standing.
With eyes closed breathe deeply in through the nose.
Keep one hand relaxed, move the other hand in front of face.
Rest index finger and middle finger of this hand between eyebrows.
Rest thumb against one nostril and ring ringer against the other.
*Close one nostril by lightly pressing your thumb against it.
Exhale steadily though the open nostril.
Inhale steadily through the open nostril.
Release the closed nostril.
Gently close the other nostril with the ring finger.
Exhale through the open nostril.
Inhale through the open nostril.
Release the closed nostril.**
(repeat 10 times from * to **)

Relax your right hand into your lap, take a couple of long slow, deep breaths
before slowly opening your eyes.

Bladder Meridian Insights

Bladder is the yang meridian of the water element.
It is also referred to as 'guardian of peace' or 'minister of the reservoir'.

The bladder meridian is the longest in the human body with 67 points along it's pathway.
Work with bladder meridian energy if you struggle to put things behind you.

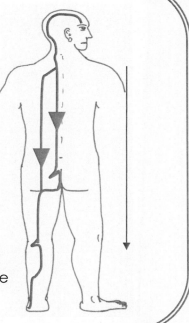

Bladder meridian runs on both sides of the body, starting on the inside corner of the eye.
Trace over the head, follow the first pathway straight down the back to the buttock crease.
Return to the shoulder to follow the second pathway down the outside of the original pathway, (midway between the spine and outer edge of the back).
Reconnect the pathways at the buttock crease and continue this single pathway down the back of the thigh, knee and calf, along the outer side of the foot to the outside end of the little toe.

With a flat hand trace the bladder meridian pathway (or as much of it as you can comfortably reach) 3 times on each side, to restore peace and patience.

The bladder is a flexible muscular bag capable of holding up to 500ml of fluid. Expanding from 5cms long when empty to 13cms when full, the bladder is shaped to prevent urine flowing back into the system.
The urge to urinate is triggered by the concentration of uric acid in the bladder.
The less concentrated the urine the more fluid the bladder can comfortably hold.

Bladder meridian energy peaks between 3pm and 5pm, but you can use the tips in this section at any time of day and whenever you need to feel calm, courageous or peaceful.

It's not the mountains ahead that wear us down, it's the grain of sand in our shoe.
                                                                                        Proverb

When you feel your next big idea or adventure is beset with niggling issues, work with bladder meridian energy to free yourself from the minutiae and dive back into the flow.

Who's got your back?

Bladder meridian energy prompts us to reflect 'who's got your back'?.

Who is there to provide genuine support, when needed, in challenging times and on a daily basis.

Who can you rely on?

Who's got your back?

Use the table below to explore your current sources of available support.

Who provides support?	Type of support	Availability

What support will you need to help you achieve your aspirations?

Use the spaces below to record your thoughts on the support you will need.

Will the support be emotional, financial, practical, spiritual or something else?

Who gets a seat at your kitchen table?

The kitchen table is where we gather to listen, share and support each other, think of it as the most precious space in your life, only the most important people get a seat at your table.
There are only 10 seats at the table, one is yours, who else are you going to offer a seat to?
Who else do you trust to support you with the next phase, project or year of your life?
Who currently has suitable skills and regular availability?
Assign them a seat at your table.

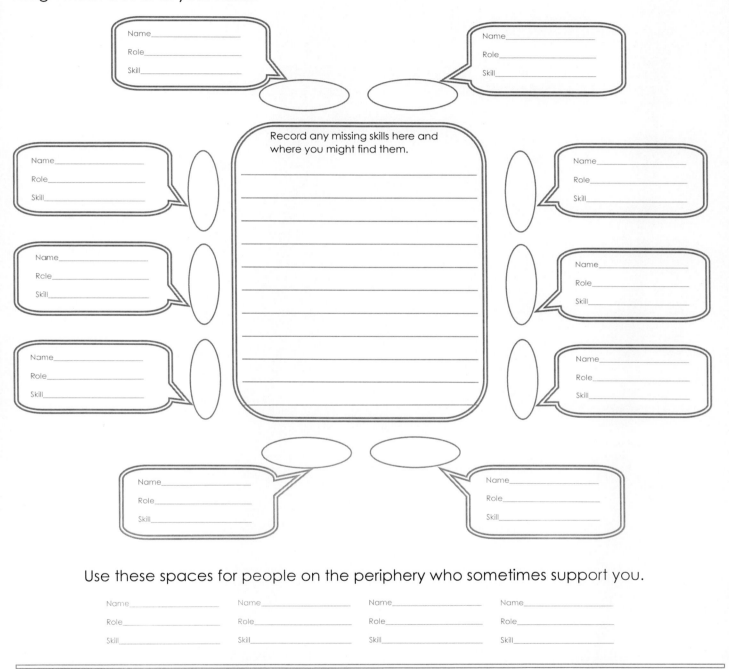

Use these spaces for people on the periphery who sometimes support you.

Name	Name	Name	Name
Role	Role	Role	Role
Skill	Skill	Skill	Skill

Keep a note here of who/what doesn't support you.

Make friends with fear

Fear is a natural response to threat, alerting us to potential dangers, keeping us safe.
Fear can be real, imagined or perceived and difficult to rationalise.
Many fears in the modern world stem from a lack of knowledge or control.
The first step to releasing fear is befriending it.
Children are born without fear, it is a learned response.
The fears you experience possibly served a purpose once, but that time has passed.
The first step to befriending fear is identifying what scares us.

> Use this space to record anything that scares you.
> There is no judgement, this is the beginning of a healing process.
>
> _____
> _____
> _____
> _____
> _____
> _____
> _____
> _____
> _____
> _____
> _____
> _____
> _____
> _____
> _____
>
> Once you have identified some fears, revisit each one individually and 'sit with' it.
> Place your hands across the part of your body where you experience the feeling.
> Connect with your feeling, breathe, then recite the following.
>
> *" Hello (name one fear) _____*
> *I see you.*
> *I know that you have been with me, for quite some time.*
> *I am grateful for all you have done, to keep me safe.*
> *Now I forgive myself for holding on to you and, with peace and gratitude, I let you go. "*
>
> Continue to breathe, giving yourself permission to release the fear.
> Once you have released a fear another may arise, record it above.
> Repeat the process for each fear.
> Be kind to yourself, this may take several sessions.
> This process can also be used when experiencing fear.

Making resolutions that work

Traditionally, December 31st is the time to make new year resolutions.
Often launching straight into the new activity, or project, the following day.
Usually, about 6 weeks later, motivation is gone, energy is depleted and the resolution is lost.

New Years Eve falls in the middle of winter, just 10 days after the shortest day.
In nature it's a time of contemplation and reflection.
A time to explore ideas, consolidate them and replenish our personal energy reserves.
Starting before we've taken time to re-charge means we quickly deplete ourselves and end up running on empty through the rest of the year.
Use the 6 weeks between New Year and Spring to build the energy reserve you will need to see your resolution through.

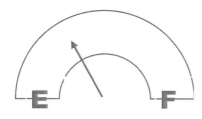

Having released the detritus of the previous cycle use this time to consider what or who you want to be, next time around.

Bladder meridian energy supports us to explore possibilities, whilst building our energy reserves in the background, ready to launch into something new, with the rising energy of the wood element, come spring.

Use the time to reflect on your values, (governing meridian) what changes might create opportunities to integrate these into your life?
What changes will get you where you want to be at the end of the next year?
What situation do you want to resolve?
How much energy will your resolution require?
What can you do to build and preserve enough?
Use the space below to record your thoughts and reflections.

Simple bladder meridian hacks

Bladder meridian is an emotional storehouse, hence feeling "pee'd off" at injustice.
Bladder responds to toxicity, urging a purge when levels are too concentrated.
Rushed visits to the toilet can exacerbate many bladder issues.
Improve bladder health by waiting up to 3 minutes, after voiding the bladder, allowing full release, physically and emotionally.

What injustices are you holding?
Are you ready to release them?   Use this space to record your thoughts.

Bladder meridian has the longest meridian pathway in the human body, spending much of its journey in the back.
Hunching, slouching and shoulder tension impede both flexibility and flow.
Try this simple and effective technique to release bladder meridian energy.

Sit with both feet flat on the floor and take a deep breath.
On the exhale, stretch the upper body tall and fold forward, over the thighs.
Rest the chest and abdomen on the thighs.
Inhale and, on the next exhale, allow the arms to drop towards the floor,
resting them wherever is comfortable.
Breathing normally allow the head to drop towards the floor.
Feel the tension release with each exhale.
After five slow breaths lift the body gently.
Lift the head last.
Remain seated.
Breathe normally for a moment before rising.

Patience

Patience is one of the most powerful skills we can develop in our own personal tool kit.
Practicing patience reduces stress, removes frustration, creates space and enriches decision making.
Recognising patience as an active choice enables us to experience, observe and empower.
Patience creates new ideas and responses whilst developing grace, serenity and objectivity.

Patience is the companion of wisdom

St Augustine

Patience requires practice.
The more we practice it, the less stressed we become.
Choosing a reaction to a situation is extremely empowering.

Consider this scenario:
You're in a shop with the goods you wish to purchase, every checkout has a queue.

Choice A

Look at all the queues
Make judgements about each queue.
Worry which one will move quicker.
Decide and join a queue.
Keep watching all the other queues.
Another queue moves quicker.
Doubt your choice.
Wonder should you try to join that queue?
Get frustrated with your choice.
Feel anxiety building.
Person behind mutters, the checkout is now clear.
Apologise.
Purchase your goods.
Leave.

Choice B

Look at the queues.
Join one.
Wait patiently while other customers pay.
Maybe put a bit of music on.
Your turn comes.
Purchase your goods.
Leave.

Neither scenario takes any longer.
Which one do you usually choose?
How do you feel about each one?
Record your thoughts below.

Try this: Go somewhere and deliberately join the longest queue.
Whilst in the queue practice breathing exercises and develop your patience.

Be patient, not a patient

The benefits of patience are physical, emotional and psychological.

Patience reduces the heart rate, increasing emotional and physical resilience and releases feel good endorphins in the brain.

Illustrated by the 'Cycle of Wellness' below, the positive knock on effects keep building.

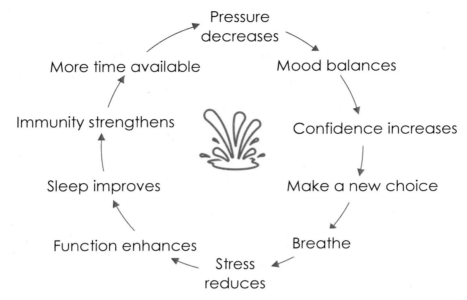

Bladder meridian season is winter, when much in nature is dormant and peaceful.
Winter is patience in action, more about 'being' than 'waiting'.
Having faith in the natural cycle of life and knowing that the next phase will come.
We are 'Human Beings' not 'Human Doings'.
Enrich the inner peace of patience by practicing simple meditation.

Try this: Check in with yourself.
Rate how you feel on a scale of 1(rubbish) to 10 (magnificent).
Find a comfortable seated position where you won't be disturbed for 10 minutes.
Lift your shoulders up to your ears and scrunch up your face.
Count to 5 then let it all release at once (don't be surprised if you yawn here).
Close your eyes and rest your hands in your lap.
Take all your attention to your breath.
Don't try to control your breathing, just keep your focus on your breath.
Every time your mind wanders gently re-focus on what your breath is doing.
Do this for 10 minutes.
Open your eyes and check in with yourself.
Rate how you feel on a scale of 1(rubbish) to10 (magnificent).
Before 1 2 3 4 5 6 7 8 9 10   After 1 2 3 4 5 6 7 8 9 10
Record your observations below

_____

_____